whole dog parenting

Published by Yellow Sky Publishing LLC

ISBN 979-8-218-08610-7
Printed in the United States of America
Library of Congress Control Number: 2022923099

Illustrated by Oana Stoica

Book Design by Oana Stoica & Vilhelem Jozsef Hunor
First Paperback Edition

JENNIFER **WHEELER**
OVIDIU **STOICA**

whole dog parenting

EVERYTHING YOU NEED TO RAISE AND TRAIN AN URBAN PUP

YELLOW SKY
PUBLISHING

For Emma, Ollie, and Azzy

TABLE OF CONTENTS

PROLOGUE

The story that laid the foundations for this book is more than one of knowledge and know-how. It is a real-life love story. Of dogs, of our city, and of each other. Our paths first crossed when I was a law student and Ovidiu was building his NYC business as a dog trainer.

WE MET in the place that was an oasis for us both, an escape from the demands and stresses in our daily lives — the dog run. Naturally, it was the pups that brought us together (and a pretty smooth line about my photogenic basset hound!).

We were fast friends from totally different backgrounds but with a few very important things in common: a love of animals, a passion for learning, and a need to incorporate nature into our cosmopolitan lives. Sitting together with our three dogs in the dog park, analyzing training techniques through the lens of behavioral law and economics (true), and debating the merits of certain breed traits, we found our happy place. In a few years, we would be a family of five and partners in NYC Doggies.

Ovidiu founded NYC Doggies in 2002 when he moved to New York from Romania, but his experience as a trainer began five years earlier, in 1997. While earning his Master of Engineering degree, Ovidiu took his German shepherd to training classes with a former police dog trainer, Luca. Ovidiu's aptitude for and love of training led Luca to recruit Ovidiu as an apprentice. After graduating, Ovidiu worked briefly as a merchant marine officer before moving to New York City to pursue what he really loves, working with dogs. With a strong background in the sciences, Ovidiu built his approach to training on traditional methods with a critical mind, adapting practices to the needs of urban dogs.

I grew up in rural Vermont, hiking with my many dogs as an everyday form of exercise and activity. When I moved to the city to attend NYU, I discovered ways to get myself and my pups out of the city and into nature on a regular basis. Ovidiu and I started hiking together and gradually began bringing NYC Doggies pups along for the fun. We were figuring out how to give the best life to our urban doggies, and in the process, we fell in love. In 2010, we officially added dog hiking as a service offered by NYC Doggies, and I joined the company as a partner.

With forty years of combined experience training dogs and running a dog services business in New York City our credentials on paper are evident, but there is more to why we think our point of view is worth sharing. Our family has grown to seven, and we have navigated the ins and outs of parenting dogs — and children — in an urban environment. We know the pain of taking a pup out to pee from the top floor of a walk-up apartment building before morning coffee; we've struggled to keep our dogs from eating discarded pizza crusts on the sidewalk; and we have left the park in despair after discovering beautiful stretches of grass barricaded with "no dogs allowed" signs. Over the years we have developed strategies for urban life with dogs that go far beyond traditional training methods.

Our perspective is new. For more than two decades we have seen more and more dogs unable to thrive in the city, and we've dedicated our professional lives to understanding why. Our solution has been to develop a philosophy and set of guidelines that eschews the owner/trainer paradigm. *Whole Dog Parenting* is an alternative model for raising a well-behaved urban pup that links successful training to the environment and lifelong care for each individual dog. We do not prescribe a rigid training model that molds behavior to the urban environment; we give parents tools to shape urban life to meet the natural needs of their dogs. This book is an adaptable resource that considers the whole picture, from lifestyle and traditional training techniques to habits and relationships. We hope that our advice will ease the process of raising a balanced dog and improve quality of life for the city and suburban pups that we love.

This book is dedicated to our dear Emma, Ollie, and Azzy without whom our family and partnership would not exist. We will love and miss you always.

--Jennifer

PART I
URBAN ROOTS

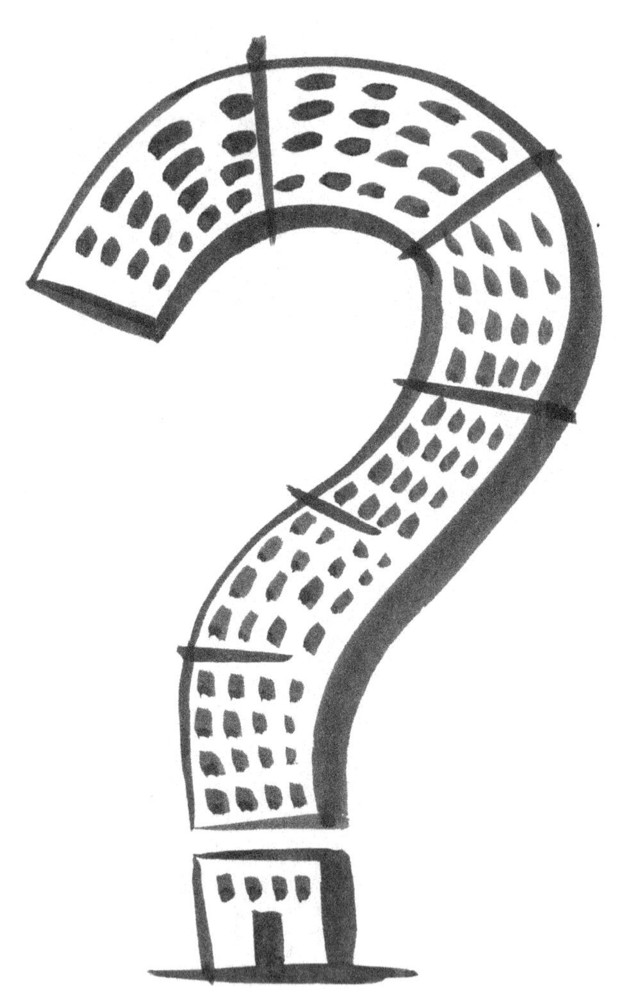

CHAPTER 1

WHAT'S AN URBAN DOG, ANYWAY?

"CHARLIE"

She lifts her nose to catch a scent, darts to a tree where the sneaky gray squirrel is leaping from branch to branch, then relaxes to revel in the feel of squishy mud between her toes. She pauses to watch calmly as a skateboarder zooms by, then with one last hop in the mud she trots back to Dad.

THIS IS CHARLIE, a healthy, urban dog, enjoying her afternoon in a city park. It's raining but she doesn't mind, she had a meaty bone for breakfast, and she enjoys getting a little dirty even though she was just groomed. Charlie is an urban dog whose dogginess is celebrated, embraced, and nurtured. She is given healthy food, lots of exercise, and opportunities to explore nature and to play with friends. Charlie is *happy* and *well behaved.* Sadly, Charlie is the exception and not the norm.

With discomforting frequency, the urban dogs we encounter are decked out in designer dog gear and learning the top-trending cult training methods, but they are not happy, healthy, or well behaved. They are anxious or hyper or socially awkward or destructive or all of the above; basic requirements for health and happiness are missing.

RECONSIDERING HABITATS

Most dogs in the United States are now living in an urban habitat, yet the expert advice-givers have failed to keep up. The literature that does address urban dogs treats them as exceptional, rather than as the norm, ignoring foundational questions about how to meet their needs for socialization, exercise, activity, and training. We think that this failure explains, at least in part, the increase in behavioral imbalance that we are seeing in our city dogs. It is time to rethink the components of a healthy lifestyle in a way that reflects the reality of the urban environment that most dogs are living in today.

Chances are about 3 to 1 that your dog is an "urban" dog. This means that in the 21st century, the majority of dogs are living a city or suburban life. And yes, we certainly do include our four-legged friends who live in the suburbs.

There are many versions of non-rural life for a dog, from high-rise apartment to home-and-garden living, and we encompass all of it under the heading of "urban dog." Despite the diverse range of city and suburban habitats, the needs and pitfalls (revolving around where to pee and where to run), are the same.

The picture of an urban dog that first comes to mind is one who lives in an apartment building with either an elevator or several flights of stairs bridging home and the outdoors. When the exit is finally reached it usually leads to a concrete sidewalk bordered by busy roads and loud noises. The lucky dog will have a nice tree to pee on, but most of the greenery is fortified behind "please curb your dog" apparatuses.

By the time this urban dog has toured the block and found a suitable — but hardly pleasant — bit of sidewalk on which to poop and pee, maybe snagging some food garbage off the street along the way, and by the time mom or dad has tidily cleaned up the poo and found a garbage can in which to dispose of it, the journey back up to the apartment where the sofa is waiting has already begun.

Of course, there are lots of urban dogs who are lucky enough to have access to a backyard. We lived in a Brooklyn house with our three dogs who shared the yard with our daughters. But let's be honest, is any city or suburban yard really big enough to act as potty, let alone for a dog to run around in? If our pups always peed and defecated in the backyard, we'd have no grass and a lot of stink. Thus, even house-and-garden urban dogs are usually taken for leashed poop and pee walks on the sidewalk.

We also see continuity from city to city and suburb to suburb in the type of activities that dogs have access to. Big group dog walks and play time in the local dog run are typical. These activities certainly have their merits, but their ubiquity

highlights what is lacking, the common deprivation that links and limits urban dogs: not having regular contact with nature.

The greatest pitfall to urban life for any dog is the lack of access to vast spaces where they can explore the natural world off leash. We are starting with this point, and we will come back to it throughout the book because the benefits that flow to any and all dogs from countryside adventures are innumerable and often overlooked. We are not just talking about exercise here; off-leash romps involve using a dog's instincts and senses. There is sniffing and tracking, rolling and swimming, listening and watching, play and exploration. These activities lead to happiness and balance.

Does this mean that urban dogs can't achieve the same things? Of course not! It only means that you have your work cut out for you; diligence and creativity are required in providing opportunities for your pup to mimic these activities in an urban environment and to escape to the country when possible. This stuff is important, and we will help you learn how to do it!

Now for the good news: the flip side of living in a more densely populated area is the all-important increased opportunity for socialization. In fact, socialization rivals natural, off-leash exploration in importance when considering the benefits that accrue to a dog's health, happiness, balance, and overall behavior.

Cities and suburbs are jam packed with fantastic opportunities for socialization, from dog runs and subway rides to sidewalk social hour and dog-friendly beer gardens.

However, navigating these opportunities for urban fun is not always pretty and is rarely easy. The same density of population that can provide fun group activities sometimes also generates sensory overload in a very unnatural way. The sites, smells, and sounds of a city can be overwhelming to any new inhabitant, dog, human, or other creature. With proper exposure and guidance — an important form of socialization — most of us get used to this aspect of urban life. In fact, one great advantage that stems from city living is the opportunity to raise a dog who is comfortable in almost any environment.

By understanding the factors that unite urban dogs, we are better positioned to consider how to meet their needs. The essence of our approach is to accept and encourage natural behaviors within the confines of the urban environment and to provide a holistic program for training that can be implemented anywhere.

CHAPTER 2

A HOLISTIC APPROACH TO DOG PARENTING

YOU ARE A PARENT.

This role will last the duration of your dog's life, and while the work changes it never stops (and neither does the love). There will be resources and experts to help you along the way as you navigate parenthood, but what you do with your pup outside of "school," starting in the early weeks and months, will be what sets her up for a lifetime of health, happiness, and good behavior.

PARENTING IS HOLISTIC by definition. Moms and dads give it all: food, love, care, safety, fun, activity, socialization, and education. The whole dog must be nurtured because ***considering physical and emotional health is the only way to raise a healthy and well-behaved dog.*** Health and happiness make balance possible, and balance is much of what training is all about. For urban dogs, a deliberate holistic approach is even more important. Pups who live in the countryside have some of their natural needs for exercise and activity met without much thought or planning on the part of Mom or Dad. The life and landscape of a city, however, require urban dog parents to consistently and thoughtfully carve out opportunities for their dogs to have a bit of natural fun. Yet, lifestyle elements like exercise, socialization, and proper nutrition are often the most overlooked components of dog training manuals and puppy guides. This deficiency has not only added to the breadth of behavioral problems afflicting urban dogs today, but we think it is a great injustice to dogs and their owners to undervalue things like fun and friends.

Our starting point to whole dog parenting is to understand and embrace dogs as dogs. Cupcake-shaped treats and doggy spas are fine, but one of the most detrimental perceptions a dog owner can develop is that her four-legged baby, best friend, and companion has the same needs and desires as a person. Fluff is fine, but the truth is, that pretty treats and spas make the owners happy, and the dogs don't care. At the other end of the spectrum, some take the pack mentality too far, treating their dog as a wolf and ignoring the differences in behavior that we should expect and command from domesticated dogs. Dogs share many characteristics and physical needs with wolves, but they have evolved in the company of humans for millennia.

In addition to considering lifestyle and accepting dogs as dogs, throughout this book we encourage parents to ***look past gimmicks*** and pretty packaging when making decisions about how to raise their dogs. Sometimes the right thing to do is obvious but overlooked because the product-driven noise is so loud. A lot of companies are making a lot of money by selling unnecessary and sometimes even unhealthy stuff marketed as the next best thing, so a critical mind is important. There are no easy fixes or miracle products; parenting is work.

Finally, we accept individuality in dogs, their parents, and expectations of what a well-trained dog looks like. An easy, one-size-fits-all solution for raising the perfect city dog would be nice, but disingenuous. No book or trainer can truthfully offer such a program for the very simple reason that there is variation in every dog, parent, environment, and relationship. When raising an urban dog — or any dog for that matter — we suggest aspiring to a more general set of guidelines. *A well-trained dog will be comfortable in different environments;* she will *know how to play well with other dogs;* she will *trust and feel safe with you;* her *behaviors will be predictable;* and she will learn and *respond to the set rules and commands that you think are important.*

In this book we strip away the noise. We offer a comprehensive look at the basic components of what dogs need to thrive and a guide to training your pup, all of which is firmly rooted in explaining the *why* not just the *how.* By understanding why your pup needs to socialize and be engaged in activity or why consistency and timing are important in training, you will be able to adapt all of our advice to the specific needs and personality of your pup and yourself.

This book should be read from beginning to end. It is not an encyclopedia. Each component of the program is as important as the next because *successful parenting is about the whole picture and the whole dog.*

PART II
LIFESTYLE GUIDELINES

CHAPTER 3

BACK TO THE BASICS, NATURAL NECESSITIES FOR CITY CANINES

You have picked up this book because you are thinking of getting a dog or because you have a dog: a puppy you'd like to raise to be perfectly obedient, a newly adopted adult rescue, or an old friend with a few issues you are ready to tackle.

REGARDLESS OF WHO YOU ARE and what kind of dog you have — young or old, cosmopolitan or suburban, big or small — this is probably the most important section of the book for you because dog parenting starts here. It may seem like no mystery that dogs need to run, play, and interact with other dogs, but the reality is that most urban pups are not getting even close to enough of these activities. Life for city dogs has been sanitized in a way that severely limits their opportunities for expressing natural dog behaviors, and the results are high rates of behavioral problems and lower quality of life.

The repercussions of an unhealthy lifestyle don't stop there. Without socialization, exercise, activity, nutrition, and proper health care, training is moot. Why? Because

> *the way a dog behaves is guided by much more than the needs and demands of her parent as expressed in a command.*

Imagine how feeling lonely, anxious, restless, frightened, or in pain can make someone behave? If she fears the place to which you are calling her, it doesn't matter whether your pup knows how to "come" on command; she may love kids but will certainly snap if they jump on her sore hip; and chewing shoes may be a no-no, but if there is no other outlet for her to burn energy when left alone all day, she will chew out of necessity and suffer the consequences later.

> *In order to expect balance and obedience from our pups, we must make sure they are healthy in both body and mind. This is, fundamentally, the first step in training.*

"JASPER"

A FEW YEARS AGO, we received a call from a woman who lived in NYC's Financial District who had decided it was time for her ten-year-old West Highland terrier, Jasper, to have a special treat. In his decade of life, Jasper had never — not once — ventured outside of an urban environment. His mom had read about our hiking service and felt that Jasper, who she described as the perfect city pup, deserved an occasional escape from apartment life with a toddler and another baby on the way. We couldn't have agreed more!

We met Jasper and got to see him in the comfort of his own home before taking him on his first hike. He was dapper and spry and, according to his mom, "perfect" with a few small personality "quirks," as she called them. He would *sometimes* snap at the toddler when toys and food were involved, he "frowned upon" being made to get off the bed, he liked to "lead the way" on his leashed walks, and he would occasionally "have a little nibble" on the furniture. Jasper's mom also requested an individual hike because, well, he preferred the company of people to other mongrels (a request which we denied). This is not a caricature, but in fact a very common and predictable set of personality traits for urban pups. Equally as predictable, however, was the amazing transformation we witnessed in Jasper over the coming weeks.

Jasper's first group hike was a bit like testing the waters without quite dipping a toe in. He displayed signs of anxiety in the car and refused to sit in the back with his hiking buddies. When we arrived at the trailhead, the other dogs immediately started running and playing and exploring, but Jasper refused to move. On leash or off, he wouldn't budge once we left the smooth surface of the parking lot and hit the trails.

He spent most of the hike being carried, but he did watch the other dogs with vigilance and, could it be, a hint of curiosity? In the car on the way back to the city, Jasper got a hold of a bag of carrots meant to be a communal treat and nearly took Jen's hand off when she retrieved it. After parking near his building back in the city, he couldn't have pulled harder to get inside the familiar environment of his apartment.

Many a dog parent would, at this point, decide that this kind of activity was not their dog's cup of tea and promptly return their pup to the comfort of habits and routine. Fortunately for Jasper, and with a little encouragement from us, his mom committed to really giving the hikes a try and put her faith in us when we explained that his reactions to the wilderness were normal, and that it wouldn't take long for him to start enjoying himself.

On our second hike Jasper started out much the same as he had on the first — a little anxious in the car and stubborn about walking. He didn't get carried this time, however, and at about the halfway mark he had his miracle moment. This is an amazing transformation we have seen over and over again with urban pups who are at first reluctant to let their inner doggy out; for the pups, it all seems to suddenly click. We think if they could talk, they would say something like this: "Wow, it is fun to be around other dogs and get dirty!" "These open spaces are a little intimidating...but totally awesome!" and "Being off leash isn't scary, it's fun and freedom!"

Jasper's moment was such a pleasure to witness. After

about an hour and a half of slow walking (and only when constantly coaxed at that), he stopped and wouldn't budge. He looked around at the other dogs splashing in the river, gave the leaf debris under his feet a little sniff, and then without warning he took off and started sprinting in huge circles. This little guy was *moving*, a wholehearted gleeful run, with all four of his stubby legs bounding off the ground at the same time. He stumbled and rolled and thought that was hysterical so he just kept rolling in the leaf litter and wiggling. Next, he splashed across the little brook (a feat in and of itself considering that his mom said he would do anything to avoid getting wet), and — wait for it — jumped over his soon to be BFF, our little Havanese hiker Petunia.

By his third hike, Jasper was an old regular who knew the ropes. He ran to the door, ready to be leashed and walked to the car; he sat comfortably in the back with the other pups, and he enjoyed every bit of every hike after that, including in the rain and snow, even leading the pack at times! The most remarkable part of Jasper's story, however, is the feedback we received from his mom. At home, Jasper's "quirks" were changing. He wasn't chewing furniture or competing with his toddler sister for attention, and his possessive tendencies toward food and toys were diminishing. She asked if we were giving him some sort of miracle drug!

The miracle drug, we answered, is socialization, exercise, and activity.

CHAPTER 4

SOCIALIZATION

We begin the lifestyle guidelines with socialization and return to socialization in the puppy training section, because it is, without a doubt, the most undervalued and neglected aspect of raising an urban dog. In fact, it is impossible for your pup to be well behaved and balanced without also being properly socialized. With limitless possibilities for socialization in cities one might expect a well-socialized canine community, but this is often not the case.

WHEN OVIDIU MOVED to New York in 2002, one of his first training clients was a mixed-breed medium-sized dog named Holly. Having met Holly in the comfort of her apartment, he expected to see the same signs of confidence and affection when he took her on their first outing. Instead, he was struck by the transformation in Holly's behavior when they left home. Holly cowered when walking on the sidewalk, flinched at unexpected noises, and didn't play with other dogs at the park.

This was a dog who was entirely overwhelmed by the urban environment because she was not introduced to it at the right age and in the right way. Holly's story is not unique, and over the years Ovidiu has seen dozens of dogs with the same problems stemming from a lack of socialization.

Signs of a dog who has not been adequately socialized range from minor things, like barking at the kid on the skateboard, to serious behavioral problems, including anxiety and aggression. By far the most prevalent and heartbreaking problems that Ovidiu has seen as a dog trainer in New York for the last 21 years are related to lack of socialization. Typically, the unsocialized city dog is skittish on the street and, in the worst cases, anxieties can manifest as fear aggression. The problem is compounded because a fear-aggressive dog cannot be easily socialized in shared public spaces.

So, what is socialization anyway? It is much more than just providing your dog with doggy friends, though this is a critical aspect. It means getting your dog used to being with other **humans**; making sure your dog is comfortable in different **environments**; exposing your dog to **new sensory experiences**; and giving your dog the opportunity to learn from and have fun with **other dogs**.

In a nutshell, socializing your pup means showing her that she will always be safe in your care when experiencing the vast and diverse world that you live in.

We explore each of these areas further by explaining some typical behavioral misconceptions related to a lack of socialization, followed by tips on how to properly socialize your pup.

1 SOCIALIZING WITH OTHER DOGS

> Misconception: "My dog prefers people because he thinks he's human."

Your pup may prefer your lap to the floor, avoid contact with other dogs at all costs, and appear to scorn the dog run, but in no way, shape, or form does she actually believe she is human. She is not a version of Rudyard Kipling's Mowgli, confused about her species identity because she was raised in the concrete jungle. In fact, while you may feel as though you are meeting her needs by giving her the human-only company and affection that she seeks, you are depriving her of one of the most fulfilling and natural experiences for any dog: the opportunity to hang out with other four-legged friends.

It is often true that the dog who appears to think she is human is, in fact, uncomfortable around other dogs. But it is important to understand that this is not because your pup has some innate sense of humanness or was just born to dislike the company of other dogs. This is a result of poor socialization, reinforced by the parent's acceptance of the status quo. Making the hard choice to take your dog out of her comfort zone will have lasting benefits for both of you.

We often get asked, "If she is happy with the way things are, why do I need to make her play with other dogs?" You will never have to force your pup to play with other dogs, but she at least deserves the chance to see what she is missing. Imagine having a child who never has the opportunity to interact with other kids. She is going to be shy and uncomfortable if thrown into a preschool setting, but would you deny her the chance to play with her peers? Of course not, because just as learning from and enjoying the company of other children is a critical aspect of your child's development and quality of life, the same is true for your dog. After time and exposure, your pup will become more comfortable, and only then will she be able to benefit from this entirely wonderful and natural part of doggy life.

Dogs are social creatures by nature, and the benefits of hanging out with their own kind are innumerable. It's not just fun and friends, it's an education and a boost of confidence. The comfortable dog-run regular will play, rest, sunbathe, and play again. She will learn that not everyone wants to be jumped on or chased, and she'll know when to take a hint. She will be confident checking in with the other dogs, learning about their day through appropriate sniffing, and she will know how to share her toys.

Socializing with other dogs is how your pup will learn the rules of the game: the boundaries and language that guide dogs in a social environment. This is critical stuff, particularly in an urban environment. Here, it is impossible to avoid contact with other pups whether it be on the street, in the elevator, or in the park, and when it happens you want your dog to feel comfortable and balanced, not stressed and afraid.

The basic idea is simple: provide your dog with ample opportunities to be in the presence of and to interact with other dogs. In the city and suburbs, opportunities for letting your pup spend time with like-minded creatures are myriad. Group walks, trips to the dog run, off-leash park hours, and even play dates are all good ways to socialize your dog. The environment should feel safe, and it is your job as human parent to ensure this by being attuned to your dog and her surroundings. We will get you started with suggestions here, but note that if you have a new puppy, you will need to follow specific guidelines for pre-vaccinated pups that we discuss in Chapter 10.

Here are a few basic, everyday ways to socialize your pup with other dogs:

WALKS: If you have a dog walker, try a small group walk. We get a lot of requests for individual walks by parents who believe their dog will benefit more from the one-on-one time with her walker. The truth is that most dogs get a lot more out of a walk with one or two dog buddies. Dogs who walk in groups of two to three get to know each other well and love the interaction. Even if it's the only time of the day they spend with other dogs, it's a chance to read the news (i.e., do a little butt sniffing), play, and bask in the comfort of company and community.

We find that it is important not to have more than three dogs per walk for two reasons. The first is safety: it is nearly impossible for any dog handler, no matter how experienced, to keep a large group of dogs safe on the streets of the city in the event of an emergency or unforeseen accident. Second, for the pups being walked, three is company, but more tends to be a crowd. A fun and social experience can easily feel more like being led in a cattle car to the street to defecate en masse, which is pretty much what a large group dog walk is.

DOG RUN: Even better than just a walk with friends is a walk to the dog run. It is common to find public dog runs in cities, suburbs, and even some rural communities. Dog runs vary in size and quality, but they all provide the opportunity for off-leash play and socializing even for dogs who don't respond well to "come." Not all dogs will play at the dog run, but trust us, they are having a social experience.

Our basset hound Emma, dachshund Ollie, and German shepherd Azzy love to go to the dog run, but they have very different experiences there. Ollie goes to read the news. He does a lot of butt sniffing and greeting at the door. Once in a while he likes to sprint in circles, but only as long as the pack following is pretty small. Emma earned the title of Sheriff at our local dog run. She likes to sit pretty lazily until someone else starts a game of chase, then she will sprint, bark like crazy, and intercept the little runner at an unforeseen cut-off point. Satisfied with her work, she'll return to an open spot and do some sunbathing until the next opportunity for police work arises.

Azzy just wants his humans to throw the ball (and he loves a game of chase, but his size can be pretty intimidating to the little guys). All three of our dogs experience the dog run in different ways, and none is the pup who is running around, always making new friends and inspiring games of chase. Yet, they are watching and learning from other dogs, meeting new faces and personalities, and constantly interacting even if it isn't always obvious to us.

If your pup is nervous about entering the dog run, make it less intimidating. Go to the dog park in the early morning when it is mostly empty, and let her get used to the space. Gradually introduce her to busier park hours, all the while using play to make the experience really positive and fun for her. This is the same approach you will take when introducing her to any new social experience that she finds a little scary.

PUBLIC PARKS: Public parks are another great resource for dog parents, particularly if you are comfortable enough to allow your dog to socialize off leash in an open setting. Many dogs are, in fact, more comfortable in an environment that doesn't include a fence and may be more amenable to meeting other dogs. Do your research because urban parks sometimes have designated off-leash hours; others never require leashes. For most pups, socializing off-leash in the park is a better option than the dog run. We'll talk about this more later in the exercise and activities sections, but even on a leash, parks are a fantastic place to meet and have a quick doggy chat with new friends. Every interaction is a learning experience.

A DOGGY SOCIAL SPACE: Though still a new trend, we are seeing more and more dog-specific social spaces popping up in cities. Parents in New York can now take their pups out to lunch and eat together inside at Boris & Horton café or become members of a doggy social club. Join your local dog community groups and don't be afraid to ask around. Where do parents in your city and neighborhood get together for some fun?

PLAY DATES AT HOME: If it is hard to get out, you can't brave the weather, or for some particular health or behavioral issue you need to keep your pup in a home environment, don't worry. You can still socialize your dog. Our advice is to get to know the dogs in your building, on your block, or in your neighborhood, and make some doggy friends. Our pups love having company at home. Sometimes they play, and sometimes they just snuggle up together. Dogs often have different behaviors on their home turf, which is normal, but as long as you know your pup and your guests, you are capable of providing a fun and safe environment. It's typical for dogs to be more possessive over toys and furniture at home, but it is not a reason to avoid play dates. Dogs learn to share, and inviting over a trusted friend is a great way to practice in a supervised environment.

2   SOCIALIZING WITH OTHER PEOPLE

Misconceptions: "My dog is prejudiced," "My dog is racist."

It is hard to believe how often these phrases are uttered by dog parents whose pups have not been properly socialized. Let's get one thing straight: discomfort with the unfamiliar is not racism. Your dog does not believe that because a person has a different skin color or is a different gender, that she is inherently inferior to you. We would have a big, intractable problem if dogs had that level of hateful cognition.

That being said, one of the most common results of a dog not having been properly socialized is a fear of those humans who stand out in some way or are different from the people they are used to seeing (a.k.a. different from you). Age, skin color, size, smell, movement, uniforms, and unfamiliar accessories like hats and backpacks are some of the more common human differences that incite dogs to appear to "discriminate" in their behavior. Even differences in personality and behavior like confidence and timidity can cause dogs to react to the unfamiliar.

The behaviors that an un-socialized dog may exhibit when she comes into contact with an unfamiliar person are the same behaviors exhibited when dogs see an unusual object in an unlikely place or are presented with a new situation: intense curiosity, shyness, barking, even snarling and other forms of aggression. The unknown induces caution, sometimes fear, and can be a source of anxiety.

Our most humiliating moment as dog parents was when our basset hound, Emma, was 3 years old. She was approached by an adult with dwarfism who loved bassets and asked if he could say hello. "Of course!" was our response, because Emma thrives on human affection, generally regardless of who is giving it. To our horror and shame, however, she barked loudly then jumped up on the man and knocked him off of his feet and onto the sidewalk.

Despite living in the city, and despite loving to meet strangers, Emma had never before interacted with a person who has dwarfism, and she reacted with fear. Fortunately for us, Emma's victim, Peter, was very gracious and over the years we saw him often in the neighborhood. As with all of the other types of people who inhabit our city, Emma got used to Peter after a few interactions, and this, in a nutshell, is the definition of socializing dogs with humans.

But here are some tips to help you out:

WHERE: Finding places to socialize your dog with other humans in the city and the suburbs is the easy part. The first and most convenient place is wherever you take your dog to be with other dogs. You will be in a friendly environment, and people in places like the dog run tend to love saying "hi" to all the pups present. It is important, however, to have your dog interact with people in a variety of environments. This means in your home, in others' homes, in the car, on the street, on leash and off leash. Because dogs can alter their behavior in different environments, exposure to different people should take place in all environments that will be a part of your pup's life.

WHO: Your dog should be familiar with as many different kinds of people you can find: tall and short, fat and skinny, different genders, light and dark, and everything in between, hyper and shy, outgoing and awkward, elderly, disabled, loud and quiet, bearded, glasses-wearing, uniformed and not! Bikers, skateboarders, hatted and helmeted, runners and walkers, suits and hipsters! Whoever you can find, the more types of people the better, but don't forget the most important category of all: ***children.***

It is very common for dogs to be uncomfortable around children — these little people haven't learned the boundaries and social norms that adults live by, and they can be unpredictable. Unpredictable to a dog often means scary. The result of confrontations between dogs who haven't been well socialized and children can be much uglier than the kind of interaction we discussed above that ended with Peter on the pavement, graciously telling us it was "okay."

HOW: For the most part, this is self-explanatory. The best way is to have the kids or the UPS delivery person socialize with your pup is to actually have them play and interact with her. The experience will be fun, positive, safe, and you will remain calm throughout. If your dog isn't used to being around children, don't bring her to a preschool on day one of socialization. Have her meet one child, preferably someone you know, who is calm and can follow your lead. The child should be seated in the beginning and should wait for the dog to approach her, not the other way around. Incrementally, you will introduce more children in different environments and with different levels of energy. Always be mindful of signs of stress from your dog.

In sum, there is no excuse, especially in a city like New York, to have a dog who reacts with fear to different kinds of people. Cities are big, beautiful, diverse places, and they provide the perfect opportunity to raise a well-socialized dog.

3   SOCIALIZING TO DIFFERENT ENVIRONMENTS

> Misconception: "My dog is a city dog. She does not like to get her feet dirty."

We used to live next door to a hair salon owned by a man with a very sweet Italian Greyhound puppy named Puppet. We sometimes brought Ollie in to play with her; Puppet was an exuberant, loving, and playful young pup with tons of energy. She would often try to escape and run across the street into the park. But as she grew up, we saw Puppet's behavior changing and noticed some rather odd habits of her parent. Every day, the parent carried her from car to salon and perched her on the sofa. Puppet became reluctant to get off the sofa even to play with Ollie. She only used wee wee pads to defecate, and on the one or two occasions that we saw her feet touch the grassy knoll between car and salon, her parent immediately took out an antibacterial wipe to give her a thorough (and thoroughly uncomfortable looking) clean. When we asked why she used wee wee pads, her parent responded that Puppet "does not like to get her feet dirty." Did she never go for walks, then? we asked. No, she did not care for them.

This is an extreme case, but every bit is true, and Puppet's story exemplifies the kind of behaviors pups learn based on the environments they are allowed to experience. Puppet was not naturally averse to being outside or going for walks; she was taught by her parent to prefer the sofa. In doing so, her parent withheld from her a world full of enjoyable experiences.

On the other hand, Puppet was remarkably comfortable in the urban environment because her parent carried her all over the city — on the subway, to baseball games, to restaurants, and on trains. This leads us to problems at the other end of the environmental socialization spectrum:

> Misconception: "My dog cannot handle the sensory overload of the city."

For a lot of dogs, this is actually true, but it is because they were not properly socialized to the urban environment. One of the pups we take hiking, Tilly, makes this evidently clear every time she is leashed to leave the apartment. She starts panting and trembling, and the moment she steps onto the sidewalk she becomes hyper-alert to every noise. She walks to the closest tree to pee and then tries to run inside. She refuses to walk any further. We know it is the urban environment that she was not socialized to because it isn't where she was raised as a puppy, and when she gets out of the city for hikes she doesn't display any of these signs of anxiety.

Socializing your dog to an urban environment often takes a lot more work than getting a dog used to a natural environment. In some cases, the process even involves working against a dog's instincts. It could be something minor, like teaching your pup that it is safe to walk across the metal grating on the sidewalk even though it doesn't feel like the ground should feel on her feet. Or, it can be something more challenging like teaching your dog to feel calm at a busy intersection when sirens are sounding, lights are flashing, horns are beeping, cars are zooming, and tall buildings are looming. On the flip side, it can also be a lot of fun — try a dog-friendly bar or café!

Dogs get the most out of life when they are comfortable interacting in any environment, and the best way to achieve comfort (i.e., being socialized to different environments) is simply through exposure and experience. With puppies it is easier because they haven't yet mapped the world into safe and scary places. With adult dogs it can be much harder, but the approach is the same.[1] Take your dog lots of places, let her smell everything, see new sites, hear the sounds of city and country, feel both mud and metal sidewalk grating between her toes, ride in cars and trains and subways, walk on busy streets and empty fields. All the while, make sure your dog knows she is safe by staying calm and keeping her engaged in the walk.

 For environments that are more stimulating than normal (for example a very loud construction site), or if you notice signs of anxiety from your dog, take incremental steps. Go to the point at which signs of anxiety begin and no further on the first day. Stay there calmly for a few minutes. Act normally and be your pup's rock. Then put a little more distance between you and the site, stop for another few minutes and relax, then move

---

1)   For adult dogs who exhibit symptoms of stress, anxiety, or fear-based aggression in urban environments, the approach to socialization is different. It involves a much more incremental exposure therapy.

a bit further away and play with your pup. Next time you will start a bit closer to the construction site, and in this way, she will get used to the noise by feeling safe with you.

That feeling of safety is what you will carry through all the different types of socialization: dogs, people, and environments. By keeping these experiences positive and integrating them into everyday life you will watch your pup develop into a well-socialized member of her urban community. And once you have achieved this, the rest is easy!

SOCIALIZATION WITH YOUR URBAN PUP IS FUN!

There is absolutely no excuse for failing to get out and about with your pup because city-dwellers have access to an unprecedented abundance of dog-friendly cultural spaces and events. New Yorkers can grab a pint at Brooklyn Brewery or a coffee at The Grey Dog then take their pup art hopping in Chelsea, visit a dog beach, even try out kayaking on the Hudson. All across the country, cities and businesses are opening their doors to dogs and their parents.

CHAPTER 5
EXERCISE AND ACTIVITY

For the first eight months of our oldest daughter's life, we had a fussy, fussy, fussy human baby on our hands. We knew that it was normal, and that our little person had lots of energy to burn so she burned it by crying. Bea was a high-energy baby in a little immobile body, but as soon as she was strong enough to start crawling, we saw an instant transformation from frustrated fuss-bucket to exuberant explorer and super-sleeper. As she has grown bigger and stronger, we have had to seek out bigger urban spaces for burning energy, but as long as we go to the playground every day, we don't usually have a little fuss-monster on our hands.

DOGS ALSO GET FUSSY because they need to burn energy, but unlike human babies, they don't ever have to go through a period of immobility. They don't have big wobbly heads on short necks; practically from birth, they are built to run, sniff, explore, and play. If they don't get the opportunity to do so, dogs of any age will suffer physically and psychologically, and unwanted behaviors will follow. It may sound obvious, but we encounter the problem all the time, and the remedy is so straightforward. We have seen a complete transformation in countless "fussy" city dogs whose frustrated parents make the right decision and start providing their pups with regular exercise and activity.

It may at first seem like the close quarters of the urban habitat make exercising your pup a challenge, but today's cities offer up a bounty of recreational opportunities for dogs.

WHAT ARE EXERCISE AND ACTIVITY?

Exercise is the raw physical activity that keeps your dog fit in both body and mind. Regardless of the breed, dogs are not naturally sedentary creatures and they require exercise to be happy and healthy.

Activity refers more specifically to the ways in which you stimulate your dog's mind and senses, often, but not always, in the form of physical exercise.

Let's look at some examples for clarification: putting your dog on a treadmill for an hour will certainly achieve some exercise goals like burning energy, releasing good hormones, and building muscular and cardiovascular strength, but where is the mental stimulation? It could be provided by figuring out how to get the peanut butter out of a toy, but of course the exercise is lacking from this activity. An off-leash walk in the park, on the other hand, is both good physical exercise and an activity that stimulates your pup's mind and senses by providing an environment that is fun to explore.

WHY ARE EXERCISE AND ACTIVITY IMPORTANT?

> Misconception: "My dog is misbehaving because she is angry with me."

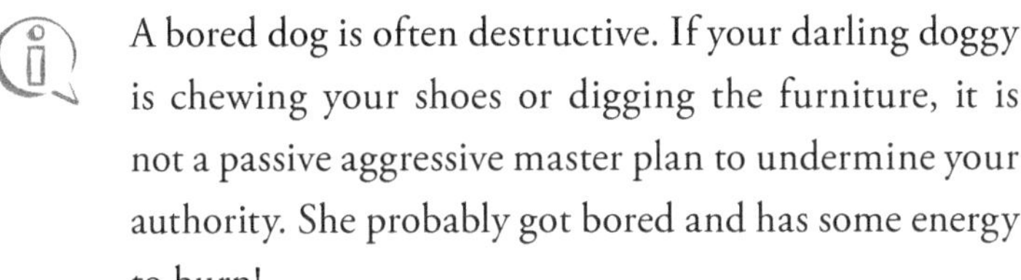

A bored dog is often destructive. If your darling doggy is chewing your shoes or digging the furniture, it is not a passive aggressive master plan to undermine your authority. She probably got bored and has some energy to burn!

Behavioral and psychological problems stemming from a lack of exercise and stimulation can range from minor mischief, like chewing on furniture or prolonged periods of barking, to really serious issues like anxiety and aggression. We have seen dog parents go to great lengths to decipher worrisome behaviors in their dogs without first providing them with exercise and activity, very basic components of a holistic, healthy lifestyle.

Like in humans, physical problems related to a lack of exercise often stem from obesity. For dogs, being overweight puts a tremendous amount of stress on their joints and can lead to a long list of other health issues. Being overweight will almost certainly shorten your dog's lifespan.[2]

---

2)	Salt, C., Morris, P., Wilson, D., Lund, E., & German, A. (2018). Association between life span and body condition in neutered client-owned dogs. Journal of Veterinary Internal Medicine.

Misconception:
"My dog is just naturally lazy."

Laziness is a learned habit in dogs. Regardless of whether she acts like she wants to go for a walk, she needs it and it is your responsibility to motivate her to move.

Psychologically, problems related to a lack of exercise and activity can be particularly sharp in dogs that have been bred to work for a particular purpose. For generations, we humans have selectively bred dogs to not only be capable of amazing feats, but to desire to achieve those feats with every fiber of their being. The recent increase in urban dog populations means that

more dogs than ever before are not performing the tasks that they are instinctively driven to do.

In this section we'll just take one example to illustrate the principle: the border collie. This is a dog who has an overwhelming instinct to herd, an activity that requires an enormous amount of energy and intelligence. The border collie was bred to run and to interact in complex and collaborative ways with her human companion and the herd. Imagine a dog whose mind was designed to constantly be aware of subtle visual and aural cues necessary for herding — a dog whose instinct is to move — having to live in a small, unstimulating apartment. She needs outlets for her physical and mental energy or both she and her parent will, without a doubt, suffer serious consequences.

RECONCILING NATURAL BEHAVIORS IN AN URBAN, DOMESTIC ENVIRONMENT

In order to provide appropriate exercise and activity for your dog, it is important to incorporate opportunities for her to indulge in natural behaviors. At the risk of sounding obvious, we are going to describe the merits of some of the most basic canine behaviors — like rolling, sniffing, digging, and barking because, in our experience, dog parents often view them as inappropriate or yucky.

We get it, and we've been there: sometimes these behaviors *are* inappropriate and yucky, particularly in an urban environment. It's really cute when our basset hound, Emma, rolls in the freshly cut grass in the countryside, but not so cute when it is human feces in the corner of our neighborhood park; we love watching our dachshund Ollie dig tunnels in the dirt, but we don't want to buy a new couch because he thinks a badger lives underneath it.

As frustrating as these behaviors can be for us humans, they are fundamental and natural activities that pups not only enjoy, but that contribute to the overall wellbeing and behavioral balance of a healthy dog. When thinking about how to address any dog behavior, it is so important to remember that ***dogs did not evolve to respect the boundaries of a controlled and humanized urban world.*** We have to help them learn how to navigate that unnatural environment through training and socialization while at the same time giving them opportunities and spaces where they can act like dogs in a natural environment.

Some of the behaviors we discuss in this section, like digging, barking and chewing, can be very destructive in the wrong context, and our approach to dealing with them is three-pronged.

First, recognize that they are natural, stimulating, and fun so should be deliberately incorporated into the activities that you are planning for your pup.

Second, when it isn't possible to provide opportunities for these natural behaviors because of the urban environment, make sure your pup is otherwise well exercised.

Third, set limits on these behaviors in the home or wherever necessary. If your pup is well exercised and stimulated, she will be a calmer and quieter dog when you need her to be. She will also learn that chewing on Dad's slippers is not acceptable, but chewing on a stick outside is.

ROLLING:

Anyone who tells you they know why dogs like to roll, particularly in the feces of other animals, is wrong. Scientists have lots of ideas as to why wolves (who passed down this behavior to domesticated dogs) roll in all sorts of stinky stuff, but at this point they are just hypotheses. Strong smells might confuse prey or predators, they might tell a story to the pack about where the canine has been, or maybe sharing in a stink is a group bonding experience![3]

Regardless of the reason why, the instinct to roll is a fact of life for modern day dogs, and, as with any natural instinct, it feels really good for dogs to be able to engage in the behavior.

We are not suggesting that you encourage your pup to cover herself in poop or dead animal smells. However, indulge her when it comes to cut grass or some clean country mud. This is the doggy equivalent of soaking in a hot bath at the end of a long, cold, rainy day outside. It feels good and it is amazing to see the joy that exudes from a pup, large or small, young or old, when given the chance to flop over in a pile of leaves, scratch that back and roll around! And, if she does discover the deer poop when you aren't looking, please don't punish her, just wash it off and move on.

SNIFFING:

A dog's nose is so much more powerful and integral to the way she interacts with the world than the human nose, that it is difficult for us to even imagine. Dogs read the news, track their families and food, and map the world with their noses. And what a nose it is! Scientists believe that the canine

---

3)   Gray, R. (June 8,2017). The many reasons why dogs might roll in smelly poo. BBC Earth. http://www.bbc.com/earth/story/20170608-the-many-reasons-why-dogs-might-roll-in-smelly-poo.

sniffer is between 10,000 and 100,000 times more powerful than ours.[4] If we analogize to vision, what we can see from 100 feet away, at a minimum, our dogs would be able to see from 190 miles away. Or, put another way by dog cognition expert Alexandra Horowitz, if you can sense a teaspoon of sugar in a cup of coffee, your dog can sense that same teaspoon in one million gallons of water![5] Not only are dogs exponentially better at smelling than we are, but a much larger percentage of their brain is devoted to processing those odors.

Thus, the importance of this simple activity — smelling — cannot be overstated. We don't know the extent of what pups learn from sniffing each other, including what human parents often see as the unsavory activity of butt-sniffing, but we know that it is a lot, including age, gender, and health status. Stopping your pup from sniffing her friends because it makes you uncomfortable is like trying to blindfold and gag your children when they have playdates. Not fun.

Urban environments offer up an olfactory bonanza, but they are rarely conducive to creating fun and engaging sniffing activities for your pup. It's certainly understandable that when street garbage, urine in the alley, and the delivery man's pants offer up the most exciting sniff zones for a city pup that her parent might find the activity "inappropriate" or "yucky." This

---

4)   Tyson, P. (October 4, 2012). Dog's dazzling sense of smell. PBS NOVA. http://www.pbs.org/wgbh/nova/nature/dogs-sense-of-smell.html.

5)   Horowitz, Alexandra. Inside of a Dog: What Dogs See, Smell, and Know. Scribner, 2010.

means that you should take extra initiative to meet your dog's needs through activities that don't have an ick factor.

Some of the activities that we discuss in the next section are specifically designed to challenge your dog's sense of smell. The all-important nose needn't be the main focus — just be aware that it's is a key ingredient to whatever you are doing with your dog!

DIGGING:

Digging is yet another behavior that is not really conducive to city or suburban life. It's always obvious when our notorious neighborhood digger, Otis, has been to the dog run. The "pupholes" that he has left behind quickly fill up with rainwater (which is really diluted dog pee and poop). Or, if you are present when the Dog Park Digger is at work, you might get an eyeful of less-than-sanitary gravel. For those lucky enough to have a backyard in the city, your pup's desire to dig can quickly turn your carefully curated patch of earth — just large enough to hold one or two precious tomato plants — into a carefully curated canine mess. It's easier to find natural spaces in the suburbs for your dog to dig, but it's also easier for her to dig a hole underneath your neighbor's rosebush for her favorite bone.

As with rolling, we don't know everything about why dogs dig, but we do know that it is natural, instinctual, and fun! For some breeds the reason is obvious — terriers and dachshunds, for example, were often bred to dig out their quarry. Regardless of where the instinct comes from, your pup may dig in all sorts of different contexts. Some dig to escape a yard or cool off in the dirt, others to make their bed, hide a toy or just burn some energy. Like with all the behaviors discussed in this section, if your pup is digging in the wrong places at the wrong times, provide her with spaces where she is allowed to dig, and make sure she is otherwise properly exercised. Some pups really need some good dirt to dig up, but for others it is as simple as having a bed that they can nest in.

BARKING:

Your dog's bark is her voice. She probably likes to bark when she is excited, to warn you when she hears, sees, or smells something out of the ordinary, and when she is frightened or in pain. She might bark when she is having fun and on the chase, or excitedly waiting for you to throw the ball. She has different sounding barks for different situations, and sometimes she barks because she was bred to. We know the hound bark well — it is signal and map for parent to follow when the pups are chasing their quarry — and our basset hound Emma's instinct kicks in whether she is chasing her brothers, her humans, a leaf, a toy, or a squirrel.

Barking is a normal dog behavior, it's fun to bark, and it helps dogs communicate. Your dog might make her friend nervous if she corners a smaller pup in the dog run and barks incessantly, so interventions are sometimes appropriate, but don't mistake this excitement for aggression.

Barking is one of the toughest natural behaviors to manage in the city, even in the suburbs because while you can physically manage some other habits like marking, chewing, and digging, the sound of your pup's beautiful voice cannot always be contained by walls and fence. Please, please, however, do not have her voice box removed because your neighbors are complaining about the noise. Give her opportunities to bark when you take her outside for walks and activities, make sure she is well exercised, address the issue with training, and if she still insists on talking while you are out of the house, try a bark collar when you can't supervise her.

CHEWING:

Chewing is often a behavior we associate with puppies (discussed at length in our training section), and dog parents who have also been through it with human babies know the drill especially well. New teeth mean sore, itchy gums and there is nothing more soothing than chewing on a toy or even on Mom. And, like many of the other natural dog behaviors we discuss, this activity can turn into something destructive in the wrong environment. But don't be too quick to dismiss your shredded shoes as part of a passing, puppy-mischief-making phase. Chewing is not only enjoyable but good for your dog's health at any age. It helps keep her teeth clean, jaws strong, and mind engaged.

Are we suggesting you give your pup free rein to tear up the house? Absolutely not, but approach the problem with some perspective. The wood, leather, and upholstery covering all of the surfaces in your home might look appetizing to your dog, and the instinct to chew is natural. If you don't tell her what is and what is not acceptable, her instincts will guide her to all the yummy looking things in your house. Allowing her to chew on sticks in a natural environment or on toys and bones in the house is not equivalent to encouraging a bad habit, it's a way to redirect energy and meet your dog's need.

HOW TO PROVIDE YOUR DOG WITH EXERCISE, ACTIVITY, AND STIMULATION

In New York we are not only lucky to have a lot of parks, but to live in a city anchored by enormous natural areas that have morning and evening off-leash hours for dogs (Central Park and Prospect Park). If you don't live close enough to one of the biggies, there are dozens of other smaller parks to choose from and they often have dedicated dog runs.

Most other big cities in the United States likewise have at least a few big parks and more accessible natural areas on their outskirts. The suburbs provide even more choices: most areas offer a reservation with walking trails within a 10 to 15-minute drive from town.

This section will guide you through a variety of options for meeting your pup's need for exercise and stimulation whether you live in a city, suburb, or rural area.

A NOTE ON SAFETY:

Exercise is an integral component of a balanced lifestyle for your pup, but it is important that it is done safely. The overriding concern when exercising dogs is ***heat***. Dogs are not great at cooling themselves because they don't sweat all over their bodies like we do, and heat stroke can occur when dogs are exercised too heavily without adequate opportunities for rest, cooling, and drinking water.

There is very little research on how much is too much for dogs, but we do know that it is highly dependent on breed, overall health, predisposition to certain conditions, and age.[6]

In the wild, animals in the Canidae family (wolves, foxes, coyotes, jackals, and wild dogs) are built for endurance rather than speed. They are better at tracking prey over long distances at a moderate trot-like pace, as opposed to most felines that stalk and sprint to catch prey. As we know, however, dogs are not wolves.

Some breeds have been specifically designed for their ability to run: Alaskan huskies run long distances as sled dogs, greyhounds run shorter distances at great speed. Other breeds are unquestionably not well-suited for long-distance running; dogs with short brachycephalic noses like pugs, bull dogs, and boxers, cannot efficiently cool themselves because the respi-

---

6)   Montague, Z. (May 17, 2017). Is it safe to exercise with your dog? The Atlantic.

ratory tract is shortened. They are particularly prone to heat stroke.[7] Other dogs are prone to orthopedic disease, like German shepherds who often suffer from hip dysplasia, and high impact activity must be limited. It is crucial that parents tailor exercise to the breed, health, personality, and age of their own pup.

In the absence of scientific studies on the levels and types of exercise that are healthy for dogs, parents are tasked with using their best judgment. We think off-leash exercise is a good choice for most dogs because it allows your pup to self-regulate. If you are walking in a park, your pup will walk, stop to rest, run after a bird or a ball, stop and rest again, have a drink of water, then continue walking. Be careful with throwing a ball or toy, however. This is great activity, but some dogs will over-exert themselves if you do not put the ball away and give them the chance to rest. Of course, in an urban environment, the everyday activity for most dogs will be a leashed walk. While we caution against leashed runs and leashed biking because your dog cannot pace herself, walks are an absolutely healthy activity for your pup. Whether you are exercising your pup in the city or in the country, on leash or off, we think these guidelines are the best way to ensure that your pup stays safe and free from injury:

1) KNOW YOUR DOG: Is she fit or overweight? Is she healthy? Does she have any serious medical conditions or is she predisposed to any? Is she short-nosed? What breed is she, and what

---

7)   Ibid.

was she bred for? Is she young or old?

2) KNOW THE ENVIRONMENT: Is it very hot or very cold outside? What kind of surface will your pup be running on, and how will it affect her paws? Is there salt on the sidewalks? Are there shady places to rest? Is there water to cool off in?

3) BREAK FOR REST AND WATER.

4) PAY ATTENTION: Watch for signs of overheating like drooling, uncoordinated movements, vomiting, or collapse. If your pup flops to the ground at every available moment, seeks out shade, digs to cooler ground, or shows signs of fatigue, give her plenty of time to rest.

5) PUPPIES: Puppies are still growing their bones, muscle, and endurance. Pay particularly close attention to signs of fatigue, gauge endurance, and when exercising your puppy intersperse play with lots of breaks.

WEATHER:

With very few exceptions, dogs are all-weather animals. They need to be exercised whether it is snowing, raining, windy, hot, or cold. If your pup refuses to walk in the rain, make it more fun, encourage her, and bring treats; she will learn. Do we recommend running your dog in 100-degree heat or taking her to the dog run when it is cold enough to freeze your tears? Of course not, we just want you to keep in mind that holing up in your apartment on a rainy afternoon is probably more about your comfort than your dog's!

EXERCISE AND ACTIVITY IN AN URBAN ENVIRONMENT:

LEASHED WALKS: The leashed walk is a sort of bread-and-butter activity for your dog. It is basic sustenance, but not very exciting. It will keep her moderately exercised and moderately stimulated, and of course the leashed walk will give your pup a chance to poop and pee. To make the most of a walk, it should be tailored to your dog's needs.

For a dog who has lots of physical energy to burn, try picking up the pace. We don't recommend leashed jogging or biking for most pups because it can be dangerous. However, the easiest way to get your leashed dog to stop smelling the roses (or garbage cans) is simply to walk a little faster and add some confidence to your stride. When you go a bit quicker and with a sense of purpose, she will understand that the objective is to move and not to sniff around and explore.

As long as your dog is getting other types of social interaction and activity, speeding up and limiting "exploration" has an additional benefit. If you save the stopping and sniffing for other daily activities like the dog park, and keep on moving during the walk, your pup will be much less inclined to eat garbage, pull on the leash, and bark at other pups — the trifecta of urban dog-walking troubles. For a dog whose only type of outdoor exercise is a leashed walk, however, it is important to provide her with opportunities on those walks to have a sniff around and meet some of her needs for mental stimulation through activity.

AGILITY: One fun way to spice up a leashed walk is to use the city as an agility course. This is especially great for active, limber breeds. Benches become hurdles, trees and posts become weaving poles, puddles become water jumps, and stone walls become plank walks!

DOG RUNS: For most pups, the dog run is a big step up from a leashed walk, or at least a welcome change. We've talked about how important the dog run is from a social perspective, but it also provides a great environment for stimulating and exercising your dog. Even if she doesn't like to play games and chase with her peers, she will probably love to play Frisbee or ball with you. Her brain will certainly get a good dose of stimulation not only from the play but from sniffing, watching, and listening to the goings-on in this doggy version of Town Hall. If you are lucky, your local dog run will even organize canine community activities.

OFF-LEASH HOURS IN PARKS: It's the city dweller's answer to a romp in the Rockies sans litter and highway noise! In all seriousness though, this is as good as it gets in the urban environment, and we cannot stress enough that if you can't get your dog out of the city, give her a chance to run free in a big urban park. ***It's not the same as a dog run experience, not even close.*** In fact, you may be surprised to see your dog metamorphosize from seemingly timid or calm into a playful social butterfly during off-leash hours at the park. Why? Your pup is aware of the fence at the dog run, and it may change the way she feels about the space, sort of like how being on a leash might induce signs of anxiety. It is very common for a dog who is known for hiding under Mom or Dad's feet at the dog run to blitz around an open park at full speed as soon as her little paws hit the grass. And oh yes, that grass makes a difference too! It is much, more fun to run on than the sidewalk or typical dog run surfaces like gravel and pavement.

In addition to a sense of space and freedom, off-leash hours in urban parks will offer your pup a much more holistic sensory experience, the kind that is fun and natural. Let her chew on a stick, chase a squirrel, or roll in the grass. Your local park may even have a spot for dogs to swim. If she is afraid to swim, let your pup dip her toes in and splash around. This kind of exercise and activity — even if it requires a bath upon returning home — will pay off many times over by helping to keep your pup happy, healthy, and balanced.

 Of course, there is one huge caveat to this activity: your dog must be trained to keep you in sight and come on command. To state the obvious, parks (even in rural areas) are bordered by roads, and roads kill. In the training section of this book we will take you through the process, step by step, of teaching your dog to respond to the "come" command, but you will still have to test the waters gradually when it comes to off-leash activities.

We recommend starting in the biggest park you can

find, or somewhere like a fenced in baseball field that is big enough to give your dog the feeling that she is free, with a very long lead attached to her. Let the lead drag on the ground and when you are comfortable with your pup's perfect response to "come" you can try shortening or removing the lead.

THE BEACH: Did you know that in New York City you can actually take the subway and the bus to some gorgeous public beaches? Did you know that those same beaches are open to dogs during the cooler months? Generally, from September through April, pups are allowed to enjoy the pleasures of sand and surf along the coast. And we don't mind the seasonal limits because most of the time the beach during summer months is too hot for pups. We love taking our dogs to the shore in the fall. The sand and wind make everyone silly, and it is a whole new world of sensory experiences for the pups. If you can find a local beach — on a lake or the ocean — you will probably unleash a wonderful and funny new side of your pup.

DOG-SPECIFIC PLAY SPACES: We city folk might not have lakes and mountains, but we can get warm cookies and milk delivered in the middle of the night, we can hear 10 different languages on the commute to work, and yes, we can take our pups to the spa. In all honesty though, these mostly ***indoor doggy facilities are a poor substitute for natural, outside fun.*** From a social, physical, and sensory perspective it is nearly impossible to match the experience that your pup can get in outdoor spaces. Smells, animals, puddles, and fence-free spaces are features difficult to replicate in an indoor facility, but sometimes they are the most convenient option, if not the most budget-friendly. City dwellers and even some suburbanites have a growing number of dedicated dog facilities at their disposal. From indoor swimming pools to bars that specifically cater to Fido, cities are giving "pampered pooch" a whole new meaning. If you can't get outside and you want to spend the money, we recommend that you weed through the fluff and the gimmicks, the shiny and the trendy, because your dog doesn't care. We would go for an agility course if your pup is really active or an indoor swimming pool (particularly for dogs with joint or back problems).

EXERCISE AND ACTIVITY IN A NATURAL ENVIRONMENT:

HIKES (AND OTHER OFF-LEASH WILDERNESS ADVENTURES)

Hikes are a kind of all-in-one super activity for your pup. They are the crème de la crème of our recommendations for providing your pup with exercise and stimulation. Why? Because being in an off-leash, natural environment gives your doggy the space to get a great physical workout while at the same time providing a diverse range of opportunities to do all those fun doggy things we discussed in the beginning of this chapter (rolling, sniffing, barking, and digging). You can tailor hikes to your dog's breed and preferences, as well as to the kind of activities that you enjoy. Here, we describe the basics of what a hike entails and how to spice it up a bit. We know it's not easy for everyone to plan a countryside adventure, but it might be more accessible than you think!

"The Basic" Hike: A Walk on a Trail

What is a Hike Anyway?

It's a walk. In nature. Usually on a trail. And it is heaven for your pup. We advocate so strongly for hikes because it is impossible to recreate the holistic experience that one offers in any other environment. We have seen so many dogs transform when given the chance to go for off-leash hikes, and trust us, they know the difference between the well-trodden path in the local urban park and a trail in the woods.

One of our hiking pups, a dachshund named Sophie, moved to the Big Apple from rural Norway, and her behavior exemplified this awareness of the urban/rural environment. Sophie did not take well to the city. On the day of our first hike with her, we weren't sure how things were going to go. She was suspicious of us and nervous. She didn't want to walk from apartment to car, she panted frantically the whole drive and did not want us to touch her at all. However — and we aren't kidding — the moment we parked the car at the trail-head and cracked the window she was a different dog. She got a whiff of animals, trees, and dirt and knew that we humans who brought her there were pretty okay after all. Her awareness of the change in environment spurred a complete shift in her mental state and, remarkably, in her comfort level with us. She jumped in our laps, licked our faces, gave a bark, and off we went. Sophie little paws hit the trail and we were besties from that moment on. The second time we picked her up and every time thereafter she was an exuberant lovebug and displayed no signs of anxiety on the sidewalk or in the car because she knew where we were taking her.

It's hard for us to imagine what the full experience looks like to a dog because they are seeing, smelling, and hearing things we aren't. The feel of the dirt, bird noises, squirrels running, wildflowers, a cool breeze and the scents it carries — these are the things that stimulate your dog and activate all those parts of the brain that she needs to use. And, of course, on a hike she can move her body in so many different ways: she can run, jump, roll, dig, walk, and maybe even swim!

Tips for Hiking with Your Dog:

The most common concern we hear from parents is, "I'm afraid my dog is going to run away," and the fear is valid. Most urban dogs have spent little, if any, time in an unfenced, off-leash environment. This often means that they have never been properly trained to respond to a "come" command. Before hiking off leash, your pup should respond well to "come," and we recommend referencing the training section of this book to help master obedience commands. That being said, most dogs feel a natural inclination to stay with the pack, whether it's just you or a group of friends, particularly if you are moving. Dogs behave very differently in this regard on a hike as opposed to on a visit to the park where Mom and Dad are more or less stationary and the territory is small. Your dog may feel comfortable wandering away in a park because she knows where you are and how to get back to you. On a hike, however, you may be surprised at how she likes to stick with you at all times when you are moving.

Of course, this isn't true for every dog, so we recommend taking some precautions. Start out with a long training lead on your dog. When you are comfortable, drop the lead to give your pup some free reign, and practice recall. Make sure she stays close enough so that you can easily catch the lead if necessary. Eventually, she will be ready for the full off-leash experience. For added security you can try a GPS tracking collar.

"The Deluxe" Hike: Add Water

Swimming is an amazing form of exercise for dogs, and almost any pup can learn to love the water. Contrary to popular belief, all dogs have webbed feet and are made for swimming! It doesn't have to be a crystal-clear mountain lake for your dog to enjoy it (although we love mountain lakes), it can be a pond, a river, or a brook. Even if it's a small and shallow body of water, your pup will enjoy splashing around. Including a dip in the water is not only for the fun and exercise but to keep your pup cool.

There are lots of opportunities for swimming that don't involve a hike or exploring an enormous countryside reservation. But at least once in a while, give it a try. One of the best experiences for us has been giving city dogs the chance to learn how to swim. Possibly our most memorable hiking moment was the first day that nine-year-old Brodie decided it was time to start swimming. His dad had tried to get him to swim since he was a puppy, to no avail. We started taking Brodie hiking, and every week he was a little bit more eager to wade into the water after watching the other doggies swimming, but he never went beyond where he could touch. Finally, one extremely hot day, Brodie started following his BFF Cleo until his feet were no longer making contact with the lake floor, and he didn't stop! We were lucky enough to catch the moment on video and when we showed it to his dad later that day everyone cried. To this day Brodie is an avid swimmer, and it does wonders for his joints in old age.

How to Take Your Dog Swimming:

Most, but not all, dogs will love swimming once they realize they can do it. For certain breeds, like labs and poodles, the instinct to swim often means that there is no learning involved at all — on the first opportunity they will jump in and take to the water like an old pro. For others, it takes a bit more coaxing and practice.

Motivation: The most important step is to be aware of what motivates your dog and be prepared to use that motivation to get her in the water. Dogs who like to chase toys, sticks, and balls make it easy for us, but we often have to be a little bit more creative. The first time we were able to get our basset hound Emma to swim, we crossed a river to pick wild raspberries on the other side. Emma is food motivated, so in true hound form she followed her nose and braved the current to get a taste of what we were snacking on! She has never been a great swimmer (bassets tend not to be because the majority of their weight is in the top third of their bodies); her little bum sort of bobs and floats above the water as she cumbrously works her way from point A to point B. But, on hot days we are all grateful that she is comfortable in the water and can take a nice cool dip. For our dachshund Ollie it is even more important that he can swim because, like a lot of dachshunds, he has a sensitive back. Swimming is absolutely the best exercise for him, but as a puppy he feared the water. We couldn't get him to swim no matter what until one day, he was chasing a dragonfly that went from the shore to the middle of a pond, and he followed! He had started swimming without realizing it, and he never looked back. Thirteen years later he still loves to chase dragonflies, but our amphibious super-dachshund will swim at any opportunity, no motivation besides the pure joy of it required.

We have taught a lot of dogs how to swim, and my favorites, by far, have been those who are most motivated by the idea that their buddy (human or pup!) might swim away without them. These pups won't go after food, sticks, or toys, but may be coaxed into the water if Mom or Dad gets in first. If all else fails, give it a try. Take a swim with your dog or bring along a furry friend who is an expert at the doggy paddle.

Environment: We have found that most dogs enjoy learning to swim and are more likely to take the plunge if a few environmental factors are met. First, the body of water should have a gently sloping point of entry. A natural lake is best. Beginner swimmers don't usually like to jump off an edge or lose contact with their feet at an unexpected drop, but they do love the mud or sand "ramp" that lakes offer to slowly wade into the water. In addition, lakes, as opposed to rivers, have quiet, still, water which calms the swimming newbies. Second, the more natural the better. Dogs seem to be more relaxed when there are plants and bugs and rocks and smells. Third, pick a hot day. Your pup will be tempted to wade into the water even if she is usually averse. And finally, bring her to water that is relatively still and calm. We've had a lot less luck teaching dogs to swim with fast currents or on windy days when the water is choppy.

Safety: Please don't ever leave a lead or leash on your dog when you take her swimming. She needs her four legs to be free in order to swim, and the risk of becoming entangled in the leash is not worth it. Likewise, make sure there is nothing on your dog's collar (like a long chain) that her paw can get caught in.

EXERCISE AND ACTIVITY IN THE HOME:

While we think it is best to get your pup outside to exercise, sometimes it's just not possible. Don't worry though, you can still get your doggy's mind and body working with a little creativity! These are some activities that we suggest:

HIDE-AND-SEEK: This is our favorite rainy-day activity, and the number of possible variations is only limited by the bounds of your creativity! The premise is simple: hide something in the house that your dog is motivated to find and give her the fun task of searching for it. We play this game in our apartment with toys, treats, even ourselves! The basic version is to take your dog into a room, show her the toy or treat and let her have a sniff, then leave the room and hide the object. When you let your dog out of the room, get excited and say a command like "go find it!" or "where's the _____?" Start basic, and gradually make the game more complicated. In the beginning, you may need to give your dog clues by pointing or showing her the hiding spots. But, with practice your pup will learn how it works, particularly if you tailor the game to her personality and breed traits.

Our three dogs know the game well, and as soon as we tell them to get in the bathroom, which is where we put them while we do the hiding, they know what is happening and become really excited. Our dachshund is a sight hound and toy motivated. Oliver usually starts the game by sniffing around, but he really likes to explore with his eyes. He particularly loves to look behind furniture and curtains, and we like to hide a toy for him somewhere that he can ultimately find by sight. Emma, our basset hound, will play this game for food only, and she relies almost entirely on her nose. Because of that we like to make the game a bit more interesting by dragging whatever the treat is (usually a piece of hotdog), across the floor to its final destination. It is great fun to see Emma follow the scent map with her nose and lift her head up to have a sniff around if she loses the trail. Azzy, our German shepherd, uses both nose and eyes to find the hidden treat or toy, but he will also often look to us for clues — a point, glance, our posture — this is the shepherd in him. He is so motivated by his people that sometimes . . . we hide Dad!

PRACTICE PARTY TRICKS: In general, we don't care much if

a dog can roll over or shake. These aren't the obedience commands that are needed to keep your dog safe or to consider her well behaved. However, the process of learning and practicing "party tricks" is incredibly stimulating for your pup. It is fun not only because she gets to interact in a new way with you, her human, but because she has to figure something out and then gets a reward for her achievement.

OBSTACLE COURSE: For small breed dogs, even in a tiny apartment, obstacle courses provide a great source of exercise and stimulation. Annoyed at having to fold and tie up all those Amazon delivery boxes? First use them to make a tunnel for your pup to run through for the afternoon and it won't feel like such a waste. If she is a jumper, use them to make hurdles!

HIDDEN TREAT: There are many versions of this game, the most well known being peanut butter in a Kong. The principle is to put a tasty treat somewhere difficult for your dog to reach or uncover. It is not hide-and-seek because your dog knows where the treat is. Rather, the challenge is in figuring out how to get to that yummy reward. The best part about this game is that you don't need to spend any money on fancy toys, so don't be fooled by gimmicks and advertising.

We save our used-up peanut butter jars and let the pups try to lick out the leftover bits; it's just as stimulating and exciting as licking the peanut butter out of a Kong and will save you the job of cleaning out your jar before recycling! One of our favorite adaptations of this game is to put a treat underneath a cardboard box. As your pup figures out how to retrieve the treat you can make the obstacle increasingly more complicated by, for example, putting a box in another box under a blanket.

A BIG BONE! Try a frozen marrow bone or ask your local butcher for a big beef knuckle. There is little as satisfying for a dog as this very simple activity. Bone chewing accomplishes a number of things. For starters, chewing and gnawing is instinctual for your pup, but she exists in an environment full of things that look like amazing chew toys that she isn't allowed to touch. Think about all that rawhide in your closet (your beautiful leather purses and shoes), those fluffy, feathered things on the furniture (your down-filled pillows), or the big sticks all over the house (wooden legs of tables and chairs). Direct your pup toward something she is allowed to chew on instead, and she can enjoy fulfilling a very natural need. Chewing on a bone can also be mentally stimulating for a dog though it might not, at first, be obvious. Watch carefully, and you will see your clever little doggy manipulating the bone with her paws, even learning how to hold it upright. She will learn to use her molars, canines, and front teeth for cutting, tearing, and chewing. And the big bonus — this activity is great for your pup's teeth.

We've provided you with plenty to get started, but this is by no means an exclusive list of activities. You will come up with your own routines for a healthy lifestyle because by this point you should understand why and how your pup needs to interact with an interesting world, move her body, and exercise her mind.

CHAPTER 6

DIET AND NUTRITION

Food! It's the stuff that keeps our doggies physically nourished and energized, yet we think the world of dog parents needs a complete mind shift when it comes to thinking about how we feed our pups. For our own dogs, we prepare meals at home, including raw meat, fresh fruits, vegetables, and table scraps, supplemented with kibble. Again and again, we are met with surprise when friends and family come to visit with questions like, "Are you sure dogs can eat that?"

FOR SOME REASON, when "ingredients include blueberries and carrots" is written on the outside of an expensive bag of dog food it feels safe to consumers, but seeing fresh blueberries given as a snack raises questions . . . and eyebrows!

NUTRITION 101:
WHAT YOUR DOG NEEDS TO EAT AND WHY[8]

When we shop for family dinner, we'll occasionally buy frozen lasagna, or instant rice pilaf, or a can of soup, but even if it's the "all natural" product, we know that it's not natural. It is processed food, and for our kids we usually try to stick to the fresh stuff. Most people we know feel the same way. So how do we forget that even the expensive, organic brands of commercial pet foods are full of ingredients that, no matter what quality they started out as, have been processed, reprocessed, and preserved for our convenience? ***How did our nutritional compass for pet food become so disoriented?*** The answer is primarily, ***marketing*** and ***convenience***.

If our dogs are healthy enough on a diet of kibble, you might ask, does it really matter? Dogs can certainly live healthy lives on a diet of kibble just as a family could survive on canned food, but if done correctly, home-prepared meals can be a more enjoyable and more nutritious option for your pup. In the end the choice should be yours, and to really be yours it has to be informed.

The most straightforward summary of canine nutritional needs is this: dogs thrive on a varied diet that includes meat,

---

8)   Recommended reading on dog food: Nestle, M. & Nesheim, M. Feed Your Pet Right: The Authoritative Guide to Feeding Your Dog and Cat. Atria Books, 2010. National Research Council. Nutrient Requirements of Cats and Dogs. National Academies Press, 2003. American Association of Feed Control Officials (AAFCO). www.aafco.org.

bones, organs, fruits, and vegetables. Dogs are carnivores, but unlike cats they do best if part of their diet comes from sources other than meat because plant-based nutrients can help their bodies to process and utilize the fats and proteins that they need.

Let's look at the nutrient profiles that are based on the most comprehensive and scientifically sound research available. The American Association of Feed Control Officials (AAFCO) guidelines break the components of a healthy diet for dogs into four main categories: *protein, fat, vitamins, and minerals.*

PROTEIN

The meat. When calculating how much protein is in a meal, scientists work with what they call the food's *dry weight*. That is the weight of the food once water is removed. For adult dogs, a minimum of 18% of their total food consumption by dry weight should be protein.

This amount varies slightly based on the dog's weight, life stage, and activity level. The dry weight always needs calculated by adjusting for the amount of water in the food — canned food is about 75% water and kibbled food is about 10% water. If you are feeding your dog home-prepared meals, fresh meat is about 75% water but 70% protein by dry weight, so meeting the requirement is easy.

Making the calculations when looking at the label on

pet food is not the end of the story. Commercial pet food labels will all meet the standard for a crude protein level because they are required to; however, the protein is actually measured by proxy. Protein is roughly 16% nitrogen by weight, so the nitrogen levels in food are measured to determine the crude protein quantity present. Unfortunately, protein is not the only substance that contains nitrogen; there are other ingredients present in the food that mimic protein and sometimes adulterate the test results.

In addition to quantity, the quality of protein in a dog's diet is very important. Quality refers to the balance of constituent amino acids present in a protein source. Proteins have a total of twenty amino acids, about half of which dogs make on their own. Amino acids that aren't made are considered "essential" because they must be eaten. The quality of protein is determined by how well the proportions of essential amino acids present in a protein match the needs of the animal that is eating it. ***Ideally, dogs will consume animal protein because the essential acids are closest to those that dogs need.*** Grains also contain essential amino acids but in much lower quantities. Because meat is so much more expensive, pet food manufacturers will often use grains as the source of protein and add in the necessary amino acids.

FAT

We all need fat and mixtures of fatty acids for many reasons including to help our bodies absorb vitamins, for cell function, and for energy. For dogs, fat should be about 11-12%

of their diet. Saturated fats don't matter as much for dogs as they do for humans because dogs have a lot more HDL (good cholesterol). What does matter are the amounts of Omega-3 and Omega-6 fatty acids and the balance between them. From Omega-6 dogs require linoleic acid to prevent skin and coat problems, and from Omega-3 they require alpha-linolenic acid (ALA) which their bodies convert to Docosahexaenoic acid (DHA). The balance or ratio between the fatty acids is important because too much Omega-6 may inhibit the conversion of ALA to DHA. Meat, eggs, fish, and nuts are all good sources of fat for dogs.

VITAMINS AND MINERALS

Among the most important minerals are calcium and phosphorus needed for milk production, growth, and bone formation. The AAFCO profiles recommend 1% calcium and .8% phosphorus in dry ingredients.

In the wild, dogs get this from bones and organs of prey, and pet food manufacturers normally use by-products, bone meal, and calcium phosphates or carbonates. For home-prepared dog food, fruits, vegetables, meat, and bones are excellent sources of vitamins and minerals, or supplements can be added as they are to commercial pet foods. The list of essential vitamins is extensive, and includes vitamins A, D, E, and B12.

EXTRA STUFF

What about the abundance of the supplements and foods

with special nutrient claims and treats? Anything marketed as having something above and beyond the norm — the AAFCO profile standard — is probably a gimmick, but let's dig a little deeper and look at some of the most popular supplements to understand why:

TAURINE: Dogs don't actually need it; they make their own.

CHONDROPROTECTIVES like chondroitin sulfate and glucosamine: The studies that have been done show only a mild placebo effect on the human parents (meaning we tend to believe that the pill is helping the dog), but there is no evidence for actual improvement in joints.

PROBIOTICS: If you want to give your dog the good bacteria, stick with fresh yogurt. Processing or freezing yogurt kills almost all of the useful probiotics. If your dog enjoys the $8 frozen treats, by all means buy them. But realize that it's more of a junk-food treat and not a nutritional supplement.

VITAMIN C: It's often added to replace what is lost through processing, but dogs make their own.

OMEGA-3 FATS: There is enough in the normal food, without extra.

TREATS: They contain a lot of sugar. Candy for your dog, money-makers for the companies.

ALTERNATIVES TO COMMERCIAL PET FOOD AND THE RISKS

The only real alternative to commercial pet food is to prepare your own (though there are also commercial options for raw or less-processed pet food). The most common mistake people make when preparing meals for their dog at home is not providing a varied diet. Raw meat, bones, and organs must be supplemented with fruits and vegetables. Not only do fruits and vegetables provide excellent sources of nutrition in their own right, but they also help to compensate for the lower quality of meat found in grocery stores today. While the protein and fat of wild animals is rich in all of the essential amino acids, fats, vitamins, and minerals because those animals themselves eat a varied and natural diet, the quality and composition of the meat purchased in a store is very different.

The other disadvantage of home-prepared dog food is the inconvenience. It takes more work and more time to ensure that the food is nutritionally balanced, and not putting in the time and research can have consequences. Even if what you feed your pup lacks only one or two essential nutrients, the result can be a sick pet. That being said, the same is true for humans — our nutritional needs are complex — but most of us manage to be healthy without having to analyze the nutritional composition of every meal we eat.

OUR ADVICE

It's a lot to take in, but in essence learning and making decisions about what to feed your dog is pretty straightforward.

1   DECIDE WHAT YOU ARE COMFORTABLE WITH

Whether you are going to feed your dog commercial pet food or home-prepared meals or a mix of both is your decision as a dog parent. If you do decide to prepare meals at home for your dog, make sure you consult the National Research Council publication *Nutrient Requirements of Cats and Dogs* as well as the AAFCO nutrient profiles for a more comprehensive understanding of what is required. The important thing is that the decision be informed and compatible with your lifestyle.

2   USE COMMON SENSE

Remember the mind-shift we mentioned in the beginning of this chapter? This is where it applies. Processed food is processed food, not miracle mush. Fresh food is fresh food, not dangerous. It is possible, and once you get in the habit, not that difficult, to prepare home-cooked meals for your dog. Meat, fruits, vegetables, and even grains can be part of a healthy diet using the AAFCO nutrient profiles and a little common sense as your guide. Become familiar with the major differences between human and dog nutritional needs and brace yourself against the marketing gimmicks that are there to benefit the industry, not to benefit you, your wallet, or your dog. Add a daily vitamin for good measure and follow the basic principles of nutrition discussed below. In addition, ***some foods that are a normal part of the human diet are toxic for dogs, so always check when coming up with a new recipe.*** We've included a list of some of the more common toxic foods and some of our favorite recipes in Appendix 2.

3 FOLLOW BASIC PRINCIPLES: BALANCE AND VARIETY

As with feeding your children or other loved ones, balance, variety, and moderation are the basic principles of nutrition that should be your guide. It's very hard for your pet to develop a deficiency if you are feeding her a varied diet. We feed our dogs something different every night, including different kinds of kibble if we have run out of fresh food, and it never gives them gastrointestinal problems because they are used to having a varied diet. In this way our dogs will never be susceptible to the kinds of deficiencies or illnesses that occur when eating a tainted or improperly formulated dog food over time.

A balanced diet is equally important. Commercial foods are balanced for you, but when preparing meals for your dog at home it takes extra effort to get the right proportions of fat, protein, vitamins, minerals, and fiber. Remember though, not every meal has to include everything. Sometimes we prepare near perfectly balanced meals for our dogs like sweet potatoes, eggs, spinach, and raw chicken. Other nights they will only get one thing, like organs, with carrots for a snack during the day. If you are preparing meals for your dog, organs are a great source of nutrients. Another one of our basset hound's favorite meals is smoked fish, brown rice, and red cabbage. Experiment and learn what your dog likes to eat, and it doesn't have to be expensive. Most grocery stores will cheaply sell you the parts of the animal that humans don't like to eat like backs and necks that are perfectly nutritious and delicious for your pup.

THE REAL NUTRITIONAL MAGIC BULLET

There is a secret for extending your dog's life and improving her health, and you certainly don't need a special food or supplement to do it for you. Drum roll . . . it's calorie restriction. Like in humans, one of the most important things you can do for your pet is to keep her lean by feeding her less. You aren't going to starve her. In the wild, dogs can go up to a week without eating, and for optimal health adult dogs can be fed just once a day (puppies need to eat throughout the day). If you are feeding your dog commercial pet food, follow the feeding instructions, cutting back if your dog puts on weight or maintains too much weight. If you are feeding her home-cooked meals, watch, weigh, and adjust the amount of food accordingly. You can also use leaner meats if necessary.

Food is not love.

Extending your dog's life by years is love. Keep her lean! She will have fewer joint problems and better overall health.

CHAPTER 7

THE BASICS OF PROPER HEALTH AND VETERINARY CARE

This is one of the most concise sections of the book because veterinary care is not our area of expertise — that's what the doggy doctors are for. Later in the book, we will talk about the experience of caring for an ill or elderly dog, but this chapter is more of a guide to the basics.

WE'VE INCLUDED IT to achieve a few things for our readers, particularly new puppy parents. It is a general introduction to why it is important to find a good veterinarian for your pup, and we outline what you can expect on visits to the vet in terms of check-ups and vaccinations. We introduce pet insurance and conclude the chapter with a short list of important ways you can be prepared to care for your pup at home.

WHY IS HEALTHCARE IMPORTANT?

The primary reason for finding a good veterinarian and maintaining proper veterinary care is obvious: we all want our pups to live long, full lives, and this means being properly vaccinated, preventing illness, and having ailments treated. The importance of healthcare goes further, however, when considering a holistic approach to raising and training a well-behaved doggy.

Imagine trying to focus on a lesson while suffering from an excruciating toothache, or not having access to a toilet while suffering from a urinary tract infection, or being expected to smile when the kids are jumping on your sore back. Health in mind and body is an essential foundation for training, achieved through exercise, stimulation, and good nutrition, complemented by proper veterinary care. Only with this foundation can training be fruitful.

Finding a good veterinarian should be a first priority when you get a new dog or puppy or move to a new city. There is a huge range in the quality of veterinary care available. The degree does not mean excellence, and we have seen a lot of mediocre veterinarians, so don't be afraid to shop around until you find a clinic that you like.

WHAT TO EXPECT AT THE VET

VACCINATIONS: All states require rabies vaccinations, but the details vary by state. Other core vaccinations (meaning they are critical for all dogs to have) are canine parvovirus, distemper, and canine hepatitis. On your first visit to the vet, your puppy will be scheduled for these vaccinations and your vet will tell you when to come back for boosters. Non-core vaccines are other vaccines like Lyme, given depending on the exposure risk of your dogs. Most day-care facilities require bordatella bronchiseptica, otherwise known as kennel cough.

FLEA, TICK, AND HEARTWORM PREVENTION: Your veterinarian will also guide you with respect to flea, tick, and heartworm prevention. Most vets will recommend some version of a flea and tick repellent that is applied monthly at the nape of your dog's neck or a taken chewable tablet. Heartworm is transmitted via mosquitos, and medication is usually given as chewable tablets, either throughout the year or only during the warmer months.

EMERGENCY/SICK VISITS: In addition to scheduled vaccination visits, you will need to see your vet for sick or emergency visits. Not all clinics have emergency services, so make sure that you have the number for a 24-hour facility. The last thing you want when you are panicked because your pup is showing some frightening symptoms of a health emergency is to be trying to figure out where you can take her on a Saturday night.

MICROCHIPPING: Your veterinarian will probably ask if you would like to chip your dog. The chip is the size of a grain of rice and is injected underneath the skin between a dog's shoulders. It is a radio-frequency identification transponder programmed with a unique number for your dog. If your dog is lost, any veterinarian can scan the chip, and — if you have registered your number in a national recovery database — find your name and contact information.

INSURANCE

Pet health insurance can be a good option, but it is not required. It's an industry experiencing massive growth as more and more dog parents opt in, and we hope that as the pool of participants expands, premiums will go down. Right now, premiums average between $400-$600 per year, but this varies tremendously depending on breed, age, and medical history. Some people with insurance receive a huge payout in an emergency situation, while others will spend more each year on premiums than they would have in out-of-pocket expenses over the lifetime of their pet. In general, premiums are much lower for younger dogs, but they don't always stay low as your dog ages. Many have built-in increases over the lifetime of your dog. There are many available providers and we recommend doing extensive independent research before choosing one. Due diligence is key here: there is no miracle insurance company that we can recommend for everyone. Make sure you ask the right questions and read the fine print before signing up.

HOME CARE SUPPLIES

While it is never a good idea to try and diagnose your dog at home if she is sick or behaving unusually, there are a few emergency medical supplies that we recommend having on hand.

HYDROGEN PEROXIDE — if your dog eats something potentially toxic, call the ASPCA poison hotline at (888) 426-4435. The first thing they will probably tell you to do is give your dog a dose of hydrogen peroxide to swallow which will make her vomit within a few minutes. Have it ready, but always consult your vet or the ASPCA hotline for dosage and details before administering.

STERILE BANDAGES — as with humans, in an emergency situation when you are dealing with any open wound that needs to be immediately covered or cleaned before receiving medical attention, sterile gauze and bandages are a must.

CONE — at some point your pup will probably have a wound or hotspot that she is tempted to lick and chew. Your veterinarian will provide you with a cone, but it is a good idea to have one on hand. This cone (or "lampshade") will prevent your pup from licking and itching her wounds. Contrary to popular belief, her mouth is not sterile.

GROOMING

Grooming is not about making sure your pooch stays pretty! It is an all-encompassing term that refers to the maintenance of teeth, nails, skin, and coat as part of her health care. Caring for the coat will help you spot any wounds, skin irregularities, lumps, ticks, or fleas; oral hygiene will keep her teeth healthy and strong and help to avoid gum disease.

With respect to grooming your dog's coat, the most important thing to remember is that over-sanitizing is the enemy. Too much cleaning damages the wondrous, complex, balanced relationship between a dog's largest organ (her skin), the coat that grows from it, the millions of important bacteria that live on it, and the outside environment it interacts with.[9]

When we mess the skin, we mess with a sophisticated ecosystem and immune system, inviting all sorts of health problems from allergies and dermatitis to more serious conditions like staphylococcus infections and the growth of tumors.

---

9)	Source material for the factual statements in this section include:

Rodriguez-Campos, S, Rostaher, A., Zwickl, L., Fischer, N., Brodard, I., Vidal, S., Brandt, B. W., Favrot, C., & Perreten, V. (2020). Impact of the early-life skin microbiota on the development of canine atopic dermatitis in a high-risk breed birth cohort. Scientific Reports. https://www.nature.com/articles/s41598-020-57798-x#Abs1.

Gould, A., Coyner, S., Trimmer, A., Weese, J. Scott, & Budke, C. (2019). Recovery of Meticillin-resistant Staphylococcus species from pet-grooming salons. Veterinary Dermatology. https://onlinelibrary.wiley.com/doi/10.1111/vde.12839.

Hoffman, A. (2017). The cutaneous ecosystem: the roles of the skin microbiome in health and its association with inflammatory skin conditions in humans and animals. Veterinary Dermatology. https://onlinelibrary.wiley.com/doi/full/10.1111/vde.12408.

Hoffman, A., Patterson, A., Diesel, A., Lawhon, S., Ly, H., Stephenson, C., Mansell, J., Steiner, J., Dowd, S., Olivry, T., & Suchodolski, J. (2014). The skin microbiome in healthy and allergic dogs. Plos One. https://www.ncbi.nlm.nih.gov/pmc/articles/PMC3885435/.

THE MAGIC OF A DOG'S COAT:

Canine skin and hair are incredible. A dog's coat creates a barrier between the skin and potentially harmful chemicals in the outside world, and it protects the skin from ultraviolet light, heat, cold, and trauma. In return, the skin works very hard to care for the coat.

When hairs emerge from the epidermis, they are coated with natural oils which minimize frictional damage and align the hair with the follicles that lie under the skin. The secretions are like a lubricant, styling gel, and protective conditioner for a dog's hair all in one. When a dog grooms herself or her human brushes her, the oils spread over the hair helping to remove dirt and other yuckies.

Different breeds of dogs even have special coats that help them safely perform working tasks in dynamic environments; length, texture, and thickness all play a part. When I take Azzy out for a hike on a cold and rainy day, I never fail to marvel at his adaptability. I am layered up in complicated gear that usually fails at keeping me fully warm, dry, and ventilated, but Azzy is perfectly comfortable in his own skin. Water and debris easily shake off of his insulating and protective double coat. At the end of the day he curls up and takes a long nap while I begin the process of undressing, cleaning myself, tending to any thorny scrapes, then finally warming up in a hot bath. My techie gear cannot compete with the sophistication of Azzy's coat.

URBAN LIFE AND STERILE ENVIRONMENTS:

A lot of people are making a lot of money by selling the idea that being sterile means being safe and healthy, but scientists and doctors will tell you otherwise. In fact, it is actually the tendency to sterilize that is linked to many of the most common problems related to canine skin. Perhaps the most prevalent of these is canine atopic dermatitis (CAD). It's an allergic reaction that can be caused by something in the environment or something that is ingested, and it makes dogs very itchy. Recent evidence suggests that a healthy microbiome is critical to preventing CAD. Unfortunately for city dwellers, some key aspects of urban life can lead to a less healthy microbiome and thus a high risk of developing skin allergies. Living in an apartment building, in a home that is extremely clean, not having regular access to the outdoors, and not spending a lot of time with other dogs are all factors linked to a decrease in the quality and quantity of important microbes living on canine skin.

COSMETIC GROOMING:

Another common and surprising source of skin problems in dogs comes from cosmetic grooming. It may seem like a good idea to clip away unsightly tufts of hair that are prone to matting or getting dirty, but it is usually counterproductive. Even when done by a professional, clipping causes trauma to the skin surface. Once exposed to the air and environment, the skin works hard to quickly make more skin and hair in order to protect itself. Grooming products likewise only muck up the normal secretions and process of hair growth. If that isn't enough to deter you from taking your pup for a clip, you also risk exposing her to dangerous staphylococcus bacteria not infrequently detected on salon tools.

HOW DO WE PROTECT THE SKIN?

Dishing out for products is not the answer.

1   A NUTRITIOUS DIET

The most important thing any parent can do for a dog's skin and coat is to feed her a balanced diet rich in protein, fatty acids, vitamins, and minerals. A shiny coat and healthy skin are generally indicators of good health — specifically that your dog is getting the quality and quantity of food she needs to sustain proper gut functions and the high metabolic demands of the skin.

2   DON'T BATHE, DO BRUSH

In a nutshell, brushing is good, while washing with soap is usually not necessary. Some specific skin and coat problems require cleaning and treatment in consultation with a veterinarian, but shampooing a normal, healthy coat tends to do more harm than good. If your dog comes into contact with something super gross or toxic, use a gentle cleanser specifically designed for canine skin. Human soaps do not have the right acidity levels. Brushing, on the other hand, should be a regular part of the grooming routine. Brushing makes you familiar with your dog's skin, allowing you to quickly detect any problems or irregularities. This could be something minor like dry skin, to something more serious like an attached tick or abnormal growth. Second, brushing helps maintain the quality of your dog's coat by spreading her natural protective oils throughout the hair, by removing loose fur, and by preventing matting. Finally, a good brushing is usually all you will need to keep your pup clean by removing dirt and debris from her coat.

3 GET OUTSIDE, INTO NATURE

The third part of protecting your dog's skin and coat is environmental. The skin is not just a barrier between the outside environment and the inside of a dog; it is also a bridge. The skin's ecosystem is dynamic and fungible, responding to and taking from the environment around it. Urban dogs need to be outside in natural environments like city parks on a daily basis. If your pup was bread for a specific purpose or climate, try to give her experiences that mimic working life.

For example, if she is a water dog, take her swimming; if she is a terrier, let her dig in the dirt. Let her play with friends and do what doggies do. If your dog was bred with skin characteristics that are prone to problems, like folds or hairless areas, you'll need to take extra care in consultation with your veterinarian.

None of us can escape the instinct to look to specialized products and services for improvement and solutions in every aspect of our lives. Addressing the way our dogs' coats look and feel is no exception. But to truly care for our pets, we need to check that impulse and look to the natural basics: healthy food, outside play, and regular brushing.

A Note on "Training"

Training is an umbrella term that includes everything from teaching your dog how to sit to redirecting your puppy's potentially destructive energy. We have divided this part into four chapters, the first being Foundations of Successful Training. These are essential concepts that, once understood and mastered, allow dog parents to understand the *why* behind each and every step of training. We've found that parents are much better equipped to successfully train their dog to "come" or stop chewing the furniture, for example, if they understand why things like consistency, timing, and clear communication are important. The following three chapters address more specific training guidelines, loosely based on stages of life and whether your dog is learning or unlearning something: Puppy Training, Obedience Training, and Behavioral Training.

Classic obedience training includes teaching your dog how to do things like *come, sit, stay,* and *heel* on command while behavioral training addresses *not* doing things — unwanted behaviors like chewing and biting, or addressing psychological problems like anxiety. There are also a number of things you will want your dog to learn that are not related to either unwanted behaviors or obedience, such as where she should pee, how she should walk on a leash, and where she is allowed to sleep. We cover these in the puppy training section.

PART III
TRAINING

SCHOOL

CHAPTER 8

FOUNDATIONS FOR SUCCESSFUL TRAINING

All the concepts that we recommend as foundations for successful training have the primary purpose of arming you, parent and trainer, with the *why* behind each training technique that is implemented later. By grasping these concepts first, training your pup can become a fun and intuitive process, so read them carefully and take them seriously!

FOUNDATION #1: HOLISTIC APPROACH

THE FIRST PRINCIPLE OF TRAINING, and one that you should be well versed in at this point of the book, is the holistic approach. It is absolutely essential. If your dog is active, stimulated, healthy, and socialized she will respond better to obedience training, she will exhibit fewer unwanted behaviors like chewing, and she is far less likely to develop intractable problems like aggression and anxiety.

If you've skipped ahead in the book to the training section, please take a little bit of time now to read about exercise, activity, and socialization in the Lifestyle Guidelines.

FOUNDATION #2: PRACTICE

This is really two points under one heading. *The first, is practice for you.* Not everyone can start training dogs and be good at it right away. It takes physical and intellectual effort to figure out the appropriate actions that you have to take, and it requires muscle memory to make those actions meaningful by applying them quickly and consistently.

The second is practice for your dog. It is probably obvious that it requires a lot of practice for your dog to learn a new command or behavior. What isn't obvious to many dog parents is that

> *maintaining fluency in those commands or behaviors is a lifelong commitment.*

The more you practice, the better trained your dog will be.

When Ovidiu consults with clients about training a new dog the first thing he asks is whether parents have the time and the will to dedicate to training. A pup may be perfectly calm and obedient when she is in the care of a professional trainer who has practiced with her, but she will only model the same behavior with Mom or Dad if they practice the same skills.

Once learned, the skills need to be practiced at regular intervals and enforced consistently in order to be maintained. Think about some of the skills you learned as an adolescent in high school. Which areas of study became integrated into your current profession or lifestyle, and which were learned then immediately left behind? Maybe you loved algebra but if asked to define a quadratic equation right now, you would be at a loss. Learning it again would certainly be easier than learning it for the first time, but it would probably take a refresher course to bring you up to snuff. It's the same for dogs.

We have dogs once trained by Ovidiu that, year after year, need a refresher course in quadratic equations when they visit, relearning the ABCs of obedience training because the parents don't have the time to practice. Ideally, practice sessions are incorporated into everyday life to the point where they don't feel like practice anymore. Remember that what you put in is what you get out, and expectations must be managed accordingly. In addition, prioritize practicing skills and commands that are essential. If your dog was trained a year ago to "come" on command and you haven't practiced the skill, don't go on an off-leash hike and expect obedience. You will be putting your dog at risk.

FOUNDATION #3: MATCHING VERBAL LANGUAGE AND TONE WITH BODY LANGUAGE AND ACTION

Not being able to properly convey a message to one's dog is one of the most common reasons that training fails. It sounds simple, right? Voice, words, tone, and body language should be consistent. But in reality, failure to do so is one of the most common problems that Ovidiu faces when working with training clients. The archetypical example is something we see every single day on the streets of New York: a dog parent — let's call him Joe — is walking his pup Luna down the street on a leash. Luna passes by another dog and starts lunging and barking. Joe tugs half-heartedly at the leash, but mostly just holds on tight and tries to walk away while saying something like, "No Luna, come on, let's go," in a soft, gentle voice. Luna keeps pulling and barking because she enjoys the boost of confidence and the adrenaline rush, and the message she has just received is, "Dad doesn't really care and can't stop me. This is fun!"

Joe has failed to match the words "no Luna" with appropriate body language and action. He does not know how to effectively communicate displeasure, and he has not trained Luna to respond appropriately. Joe should have practiced getting Luna's attention with a sharp "hey" tough posture, and when necessary, a snap of the leash. Voice, words, body language, and action are congruent.

Another very common (and seriously problematic) incarnation of this mistake is when a dog parent pairs "no" with physical affection. It sounds so clearly contradictory, but we see this most often when unwanted behavior is linked to agitation: when an aggressive dog bites, when a nervous dog shakes and cowers, or when an excited dog jumps. In all three scenarios, the common mistake we see is parents trying to stop the unwanted behavior by "calming" or "soothing" their pup.

Our friend Diane has a yellow lab named Silvie and their story is a good illustration of this problem. Silvie is usually a calm and balanced pup who loves long hikes, snuggles, and play. But Silvie lives in Vermont and she gets left behind whenever Diane comes to NYC for a visit because Silvie cannot handle riding in the car. She shakes, whines, pants, and drools when in the car – all signs of a dog with slight anxiety issues. On a recent visit to Vermont, we noticed that Silvie exhibited the same behaviors when the fireplace started crackling and hissing. Diane sat next to her, stroked her gently, repeated the words, "It's okay," and closed the fireplace doors. We asked if that's the same approach Diane took when Silvie started showing signs of anxiety in the car years earlier and our suspicions were confirmed. The answer was yes. The message consistently received by Silvie was, "My fears are warranted, and mom is encouraging my behavior with affection when I pant and shake." A better approach would have been for Diane to stay calm without rewarding the behaviors and take incremental steps to inspire confidence in Sylvie that we discuss in Chapter 11.

A dog's understanding of specific words is extremely limited; far more important than the words themselves is tone. If praising your dog for good behavior, don't say "good girl" in a whisper or neutral voice. Be excited about it because the message will be much more impactful. Likewise, whatever word or sound you choose to express displeasure should be said with a firm, displeased tone and, importantly, paired with appropriate posturing. Dogs decipher messages by reading body language so remember that incongruence between body language and tone will confuse your pup. If communicated at the proper time and consistently in the proper context, the message will be clearly received and effective. This takes us to our next principle.

FOUNDATION #4: CONSISTENCY

This principle carries forward the theme of clearly communicating with your dog and is really quite straightforward: unwanted behavior or the failure to follow a command must elicit an appropriate, consistent response from you every single time it happens.

Failure to be consistent is something that anyone who has been to a dog park has witnessed. The typical situation usually involves a cast of characters and the command "come." Mom decides it's time to leave so she walks towards the gate and calls, "come Pepper, let's go!" Pepper is in the middle of creating a masterpiece — a hole in the ground for the ages — and he doesn't even register Mom's voice. Mom pipes up a little and repeats the command. This time Pepper hears her, but he is just too busy to care. Mom starts to get frustrated, moves towards Pepper and says "Pepper come, come! COME!!!" Pepper sees Mom approaching and the game is ON. He sprints away and pretty soon has a gang of buddies chasing after him. Now he is just having way too much fun to even consider leaving the dog park. Mom gets exasperated, yells come a few more times, then starts cursing and chasing the pack of dogs while a few more dog run patrons get involved by trying to catch the little guy.

Pepper's mom set them both up for failure. She said "come" when it was unlikely to be listened to because he has not yet been trained to have a dependent "come" response in the very distracting environment of the dog run. Once Pepper heard "come" and failed to respond, Mom should have recognized her mistake, played with Pepper a bit longer and taken the first opportunity to grab Pepper's collar and take him out of the park. Training Pepper to come in the dog run will be a multi-step process that we cover in the obedience training section later on. The takeaway here is that if you cannot elicit the response you want when asking your pup to do something — or impose consequences for not listening — don't ask. You risk teaching her that she doesn't have to take you seriously and you don't really mean what you say.

FOUNDATION #5: TIMING

The principle of timing is, in fact, a facet of consistency but is so important that it requires its own section here. Positive rewards, communications of displeasure, and enforcement must be applied ***immediately*** and in ***the proper context*** to have clear meaning for your dog. You may have mastered your communications — a perfectly stern "hey!" and a perfectly cheerful "good girl!" — but if you wait too long, you will not have communicated a clear message.

Dogs are incredibly sensitive animals and can be acutely attuned to their parents by reading facial expressions, looking for signs of excitement or displeasure, and waiting for commands. But dogs live in the now, not in the five minutes from now, not in the five minutes ago. The Now. This means that if you are going to reward your pup for coming on command, you cannot finish your phone conversation then say, "Good girl Lola!" The praise must come as soon as she sits at your feet, for example. The same holds true for disobedience or unwanted behavior.

A common mistake we see is parents expressing displeasure to their puppy for peeing or pooping in the house when they find the mess. If you didn't catch the act, you are too late. The same thing applies for any destructive or aggressive behaviors towards another dog. As soon as Mom or Dad takes the time to check in with the other dog's parent or survey the damage, the moment for meaningful communication has been missed. Sometimes this even means ignoring what other dog parents in the park are expecting of you.

When our daughter was eighteen months old, we were at the playground and for the very first time, she had the courage to slide down the big slide all by herself. As Bea was nearing the bottom, another parent approached us to say that our daughter had pushed her child earlier that morning. It was very obvious that she expected us to scold Bea in some way. Imagine if at that moment, when Bea was full of pride and joy for having made it down the slide, we met her at the bottom and told her she was a bad girl for doing something that, to a one year old, was an eternity ago? No, when Bea reached the bottom of the slide, we picked her up, hugged her and told her how proud we were that she had conquered her fears. Later that afternoon when we saw her try to push her friend, we used the opportunity to immediately intervene and tell her that pushing is unkind. The timing and the context were appropriate.

The dog/toddler analogy can only be taken so far because as soon as human kids learn to talk and communicate effectively with words, parents can start reflecting on behavior that occurred hours, even days earlier. The same will never be true for a dog because dogs speak a different language all together.

It is important to note here that when a reward or enforcement is given too late it usually isn't a matter of hours or even minutes, but of seconds. Immediate means right now.

> *If the opportunity to enforce or reward is missed, move on. Recreate the situation when possible and be ready this time to provide the appropriate response, which is something we cover in the following chapters.*

FOUNDATION #6: ATTENTION

The first thing Ovidiu says when practicing commands with any dog that isn't fully focused on him is the dog's name. This is the most effective and direct way to get your pup's attention, and attention you must have. It sounds obvious, but it is another common mistake people make when demanding obedience from their dog. If she is not looking at you attentively, alert, and ready to receive information, you will not get the response you are looking for. We've seen dogs scolded for failing to respond to a command when it was so clear that they either didn't hear or were too distracted to notice that Mom or Dad was asking something of them. This not only seems unfair, but it's confusing to any dog. By not having her attention you risk blurring the rules, expectations, and consistency you have worked hard to establish.

In addition, it is also your job to always be looking for signs of stress or fatigue. Imagine how hard it would be for your pup to enthusiastically obey your commands when she is nervous about the construction next to the park, or exhausted from a long training session. You want your pup to be relaxed and alert so that she can do what you ask and get the reward. You want to set her up for success.

FOUNDATION #7:
NOT ALL DOGS ARE ALIKE — UNDERSTANDING MOTIVATION, INCENTIVES, AND CONSEQUENCES

Any person or manual that suggests they hold the key to a flawless one-size-fits-all training formula is full of baloney because of a very simple fact: every single dog is different. It is your job to be attuned to your pup, to adapt to what is working and what isn't, and to do this well you need to understand what motivates her. What will she do anything for? What drives her and what does she really dislike? We think that answering these questions is one of the most fun aspects of training a pup and answer them you must! As examples, we will use our own three pups because they are very different from one another and together cover almost the entire range of motivating sources.

Azzy, our German shepherd, is motivated in descending order of importance by 1) pleasing Dad, 2) physical activity, 3) food. "Good boy" is music to Azzy's ears and he will do the seemingly impossible if asked to do so by Ovidiu. Ideally for Azzy, following commands will be interspersed with getting to chase a ball or jump for a stick. The reward for learning something new or practicing known commands is simple — it's praise, play, and treats.

Ollie the dachshund is motivated by 1) toys, 2) food, 3) affection. A new stuffed animal, squeaky toy, or tennis ball is crack for Ollie. The nature of play for him, however, is different than it is for Azzy. Azzy plays with and for his humans — if Mom or Dad is not engaged with him, it's no fun. Therefore, interactive play works well for practicing commands with Azzy. Ollie on the other hand, is a hound through-and-through. He will sometimes retrieve a ball for us, but his preference is to chase and kill, i.e., run away with the toy and destroy it, shred it, unstuff it, or pop the squeaker. This is not an activity that can be easily interrupted in the course of practicing commands. Moreover, showing Ollie a new stuffed toy before practicing commands would be like giving a kid ten cups of coffee and then expecting them to sit still while you review multiplication tables. So, we use Ollie's second favorite motivator when practicing commands: treats.

Basset hound Emma is primarily motivated by food. She is secondarily motivated by food. And, she is tertiarily motivated by food. If obtaining something delicious to eat is a possible reward, she will do anything you ask. The inverse is also true; if in the presence of something edible, almost nothing will deter her from being a troublemaker. Unsupervised, Emma has chewed through a dashboard, a car console, three suitcases, a kitchen cabinet, garbage bins, and tote bags for the tiniest morsels of food. As a puppy Emma took her first swim to reach the opposite bank of a river where she enjoyed eating raspberries from the bushes. You get the picture. It's all about the nose and the belly for our scent hound, no decryption required.

Knowing breed traits is often very helpful in decoding what motivates a dog so we've included an appendix at the end of this book for reference, with information about some of the most commonly owned breeds. More importantly, however, pay attention and experiment with different incentives. It's a fun learning process for you and your pup.

FOUNDATION #8: DO NOT HUMANIZE YOUR DOG'S EXPRESSIONS AND BEHAVIORS

Your dog may be your baby, you may move heaven and earth for her, give up house and home for her, share your bed, feed her with a spoon, even love her more than some human family members. But please remember that she is a dog. We don't mean "just" a dog. We mean a dog in all her doggy glory. Dogs are amazing creatures, and we do them a tremendous disservice by personifying them.

We've all met dog parents who carry a whiff of superiority because they look deep into their pup's soulful eyes and find subtle human emotions like regret and shame. In fact, this undermines the beauty and complexity of actual canine behaviors and communications. It can also lead your dog to feel seriously confused.

Something we hear a lot is that Mom or Dad returns home from work at the end of the day to find a poop on the floor, or a hole in the couch, or the garbage scattered. One of our clients had a dog named Hudson who loved to chew shoes. Whenever Dad came home to find a new shoe destroyed, he would punish Hudson with tough words and a tap on the nose, but the problem persisted. Dad explained to us that Hudson knew what he had done. Dad would open the door to find Hudson in the corner of the kitchen with head hanging, feeling ashamed or guilty for doing the deed three hours ago. Wrong.

Hudson's head may be hanging, and he may be cowering in the corner, but it is not out of shame or guilt. Hudson, of course, did not know what he was being corrected for because from the time he chewed up the shoes he had done the following: had a drink of water, chewed on a bone, taken a nap, had another drink of water, sat at the door listening for footsteps, taken another nap, chewed some toys, and sat at the door again. The most likely explanation for Hudson's behavior is that he is responding to Dad's body language. If Dad opens the door, sees a mess, and becomes angry, Hudson responds. Sometimes the situation happens on such a regular basis that all it takes is Dad opening the door and a learned response is triggered. Hudson greets Dad with head lowered because every time Dad comes home Hudson gets yelled at, so he expects it.

The anthropomorphizing that has occurred here stems from the fact that adult humans will sit and ruminate on something they did that makes them feel guilty. Minutes, hours, days, even years later it is sometimes possible to detect this guilt through body language. Dad has projected this human behavior onto Hudson, but dogs live in the now. Do they remember things? Absolutely. But they do not associate memories with shame or guilt.

What a dog is thinking about when you walk in the door — and the reason we say that personification is a disservice to the intellect of your dog — is you, Mom or Dad. Your pup has an acute ability to watch your every move, to listen, smell, detect where you have been and what kind of mood you are in. She is attuned to you in a way your human baby probably never could be.

Another common example of humanizing dog behavior that we see is "revenge accidents." The story is usually something like this: Dad takes away Kato's new bone because it is staining the carpet, and when Dad gets home from the store later, he discovers that Kato has peed on his shoes. The vindictive little fellow has taken revenge! Or, we often hear complaints like this: "When I stay out too long, Lola becomes angry and chews my shoes." "Every time I get home from a long work trip Piper poops in the house to tell me she is unhappy about it."

We suggest that before you jump to the conclusion that your dog is acting out of revenge (an interpretation that has no constructive outcome for your pup), you consider an alternative and more practical possibility. The explanation for this type of behavior varies from dog to dog and parent to parent. Perhaps Kato is stressed, in which case Dad's first course of action should be to identify the stressor. It could be separation anxiety, which is common among dogs who have accidents in the house when they are left alone. Maybe Lola didn't get enough exercise because Dad was gone during her usual evening walk period, and the energy was released by chewing on his shoe. And it could be that Piper poops in the house because her routine has been disrupted due to Mom's travel. Boredom, anxiety, overabundance of energy, and not understanding the rules are all realistic possibilities with practical solutions that can be implemented to mitigate the unwanted behavior.

> *By maintaining a dog's perspective, you are more likely to be able to productively deal with any behavioral issues,*

and you'll save your pup a lot of confusion. In order to get in the habit of understanding how dogs think, feel, behave, and react, we suggest practicing a bit of self-reflection at moments when you might otherwise be imposing human emotions onto your dog. If you find yourself face-to-face with a pup who looks guilty, ask what kind of messages you are communicating to her in that moment. Is your body language relaxed or tense? Are you using a displeased tone of voice? Did you walk into the house expecting a mess? Dogs have evolved for millennia to be supremely attuned to the human beings whom they depend on for survival, so remember that

> *more often than not, the way your dog is looking at you is a reflection of the way you are looking at her.*

FOUNDATION #9: BE THE BOSS

We often meet dog parents whose lovely, normally well-mannered pup, like Lhasa Apso Pippa, really doesn't like to be told to get off the bed (for some dogs it's getting into the car or out of the kitchen). Pippa's parents explained to us that they stopped asking her to get off the bed because they couldn't bear to hear her groans of displeasure — that and the fact that she nipped at them when asked! Mom and Dad never enforced the rules both because they were afraid of being bitten and because they didn't want to deny Pippa pleasures that were clearly important to her.

The first and biggest mistake is obvious: rather than deal with the first signs of aggression, Mom and Dad took a non-confrontational approach and the habits quickly became more ingrained. The second mistake was to let Pippa dictate the rules based on her wants and wishes. We have absolutely no problem allowing pups on the bed or sofa or whatever it may be, and we aren't asking you to deny your own pup these comforts. What we do suggest, however, and what we told Pippa's parents, is that they need to be the boss. This means that if they want to allow Pippa on the bed, they should invite her onto the bed, and then they should tell her when to get off.

The rules about things like furniture do not have to be rigid. By this we mean that it is perfectly fine to want your dog to be cozied up next to you on the sofa sometimes and not at others. It is much more important, indeed critical, that you set the terms and your dog does what you ask. You are consistent in being the boss and expecting your dog to listen to what you ask of her, and you should not be met with aggression or even disobedience. The rules of the house cannot be dictated by your pup — as cute as this sounds — because you open yourself up to a world of bad habits that can become ingrained aggressive behaviors.

FOUNDATION #10: CUTE PUPPY BEHAVIORS ARE OFTEN NOT CUTE ADULT DOG BEHAVIORS

When you bring home a new puppy, you are beginning a lifelong, cumulative training process that starts from day one. Not only are you committing to caring for your dog through every stage of life, you are establishing foundations for good behavior that will endure from puppyhood to old age. This means using a little foresight to consider what behaviors you want to encourage and what behaviors you want to discourage.

Zuzu is a German shepherd-mix puppy who started out as a teeny little fluffball but is growing at a supersonic pace. His energy used to be really cute, but it was left unchecked and now many of Zuzu's fun puppy behaviors have become the serious problematic behaviors of a big dog. Zuzu knocks over the grandchildren when he jumps up on them, and every morning Mom and Dad wake up to a new mess, another household object destroyed. The consequence for Zuzu is that now he remains isolated during the day when the grandkids are around, and when he is given free reign of the house at night everyone is asleep and his destructive chewing is exacerbated. It's a lose-lose situation for both dog and parents.

Understanding that cute puppy behaviors are often not cute adult dog behaviors is just one more aspect of raising a dog that requires you, the dog parent, to consider the big picture. Having a lifelong perspective is the only fair approach for your dog because it provides clarity and consistency, and the result for you will be a well-behaved pup.

1
2
3

CHAPTER 9

PUPPY TRAINING

The importance of dedicating time and energy to training your puppy cannot be overstated. The clock starts ticking as soon as you bring her home, and your responsibility is immense. But don't be misled by the use of the word "training" here. This is not the time when you will be teaching your puppy to sit, stay, and come. From birth to 6 months — by far the most important window of that being 7-16 weeks — your puppy will be learning much, much more important things. She will be learning about the world and how to feel safe in it, to be curious and comfortable in different environments, how to interact with dogs of different ages and personalities, and she will be learning to understand you and your language.

PUPPY TRAINING can be roughly divided into categories of ***socialization, learning language*** (she yours and you hers), ***housetraining*** (where to poop and pee), and the ***formation of good habits*** (how to play, what to chew). We'll take each in turn beginning with socialization because it is the most important and most time sensitive component of puppy training.

THE ROAD MAP

0-7 WEEKS: Puppy is with mom and siblings, nursing. Puppies are weaned at 7 or 8 weeks, and this is the time that most people will bring home a new puppy.

7-16 WEEKS: Socialization. Socialization. Socialization. This is the window of opportunity to properly socialize your puppy in order to ensure that she is balanced and friendly for the rest of her life. She is not yet fully vaccinated so social interactions take place in a controlled environment. Housetraining and play are also taught during this period. Within this window, the ***most critical period is 7-12 weeks.***

4-6 MONTHS: Puppy has completed vaccinations and can safely interact in more environments like the dog run. Ideally puppy will be housetrained and have a pretty good grasp of the house rules, but this is a buffer period. Some pups will be ready to start obedience commands. Parents continue practicing play, communications, and skills with puppy like walking on the leash.

FOOD, WATER AND SCHEDULE: In the beginning, your puppy should not be left alone for more than 2-3 hours, and this will gradually increase to 3-4 hours. Your puppy should have water available at all times. She will eat at least 3 times per day until she is six months old, at which time you will cut back to twice per day. When she is fully grown, she can eat once per day.

PEN: Until she is housetrained and can be safely left in your home without supervision, your puppy will stay in an enclosed area with food, water, bed, and wee wee pad when she is alone.

PUPPY TRAINING: SOCIALIZATION

City dwellers, there are a lot of things made more difficult by the urban environment, but puppy socialization is not one of them. The diverse and exciting world to which your puppy needs to be introduced is literally at your doorstep, and This Is It. This is the only chance you will have to lay the groundwork for a properly socialized dog.[10] This means a dog who isn't aggressive or anxious, who plays well with other dogs, who isn't afraid of different environments and stimuli, and who adjusts easily to new surroundings and situations. Everything else, from housebreaking to obedience training, can be addressed in older puppyhood and adulthood. Why? Because between 8 and 16 weeks your puppy's brain is going through a rapid period of neural development. Also known as the "critical" or "imprinting" period, this is when your puppy will learn, through proper exposure, that the world is a diverse and interesting place and that with you as her guide she can experience things in a safe and comfortable way. Improper or lack of exposure will result in the opposite — the development of fear.

____

10)   Scott, J.P. (January, 1958). Critical Periods in the Development of Social Behaviors in Puppies. Psychosomatic Medicine; Freedman, D.G., King, J.A., Elliott, O. (1961) Critical period in the social development of dogs. Science; Howell, T., King, T., Bennett, P. (2015). Puppy parties and beyond: the role of early age socialization practices on adult dog behavior. Veterinary Medicine (Auckland, N.Z.).

Puppy socialization includes getting used to *interacting with other dogs and people,* being *exposed to city noises and environments*, becoming comfortable with *being handled*, and getting used to "unnatural" things like *wearing a collar and walking on a leash*.

The key to proper socialization is to present everything to your puppy in a safe and comfortable environment. You are going to be Curator and Guide, with the goal of exposing your puppy to as many situations, environments, people, and dogs as possible without introducing feelings of fear or anxiety. The connections forming in your puppy's brain at this point will be positive — new things shouldn't feel scary, they should be interesting. You are laying the foundations here for a grown dog who is confident and comfortable.

As your puppy grows older, she will of course be confronted with situations that are less than friendly or comfortable. She will encounter an aggressive dog, an unfriendly person, and unpleasant noises. But because she was properly socialized between 8-16 weeks, she will face new and uncomfortable situations in a calm and balanced way. She will respond to your commands because she trusts that you will keep her safe, and she will not react with anxiety or fear.

SOCIALIZATION WITH OTHER DOGS

Your puppy is not yet ready to go to the dog park because she is not fully vaccinated, but psychologically, she absolutely needs to be socializing. She is going to learn what is acceptable to other dogs and what isn't, she is going to learn what play looks like, and she is going to learn that different dogs have different personalities. She is going to become a social creature. It is your job at this important stage in your puppy's life to curate such social interactions for her by providing a safe and friendly environment.

Playdates in a clean and safe space with dogs that you know and trust are the best idea. The dogs should be healthy and, importantly, friendly. As we mentioned in the introduction to this section, we do not want to present any situations to the puppy that will cause her to be fearful. You'll want your puppy to meet dogs of different friendly personalities and ages.

EXAMPLE #1, PUPPY PLAYDATE

Lola is a 12-week-old lab mix. She has tons of energy and loves to chew. Lola visits the neighbor frequently, a six-month-old cockapoo named Emmy. You know Emmy's parent and have made sure that Emmy is not sick before scheduling a visit. Emmy is a bit bigger than Lola, but they are well matched in energy level. Emmy loves to play with Lola, but gently corrects Lola by posturing without biting when Lola chews her ears.

EXAMPLE #2, ADULT DOG MEETING

Lola meets 7-year-old German shepherd, Azzy. Azzy is much bigger than Lola, but it is a safe interaction because Azzy is calm in the house and plays gently with Lola by lying on the ground and letting her take the lead. When Lola jumps on him, he vocalizes his displeasure and moves away. Lola likes to curl up next to Azzy for a nap, and he doesn't mind.

Older dogs can be great teachers for puppies but be very cautious. They often have less tolerance for the simple reason that they suffer from more bodily aches and pains, and they are sometimes losing eyesight and hearing.

Your puppy should be interacting with other dogs every single day, as often as possible. Don't forget that during this period you are setting her up for a lifetime of fun with doggy friends!

SOCIALIZING TO DIFFERENT ENVIRONMENTS AND PEOPLE

Exposing your puppy to different environments, stimuli, and people is a bit more straightforward than doggy play dates because you don't have to screen for illness and temperament. Just get your puppy out into the world! Experience as many sights, sounds, smells and personalities as possible. Take her on the subway, in the car, to quiet trails, and noisy parks. Let her see skateboarders and bikers, motorcycles, cars, and trucks. Take her to the ocean, the pool, out in the rain, and out in the snow. Introduce her to your friends and neighbors, to children, and to elderly people. Have your puppy meet the mailman and the bus driver, and people of every size and color. All the while, in every new situation, make sure your puppy feels safe. You will be a calm and confident guide.

One of the dogs we walk, Wallace, spent the first five months of his life at his home on Long Island. He had a loving, nurturing, fun family, but was not socialized with anybody or anything outside of the home. The result is truly distressing. Wallace is a sweet dog who loves to play, but he cannot cope with the urban environment. He trembles, pants, and pulls the leash on walks.

What do you do if your puppy shows any of these signs of anxiety when interacting with new environments or people?

It is your job to incrementally get her used to whatever it is that is making her nervous, and to **be her rock**. It's okay to let her lean against you for comfort, but don't pet her. Instead stay calm and take her to the closest point at which she begins to show anxiety. For example, if she is afraid of skateboarders, hangout at the park near the skateboarders, but on the first day only go to the outskirts of the park where your pup starts to look nervous. Stay there a few minutes and relax. Then move a bit further away and engage your pup in play. Repeat the process for a few days or as long as it takes for your pup to feel relaxed, getting closer and closer to the stress-inducing stimuli each day. Through this incremental process, as long as you remain calm and engaging, she will become comfortable and well socialized.

SOCIALIZING TO HANDLING AND GEAR

In addition to getting your puppy comfortable with different people, places, and dogs, you need to make her comfortable with different physical sensations. This means that she gets used to wearing a collar, walking on a leash, and being physically handled.

As soon as you bring your little pup home, you should be handling her a lot and in many different ways — not just by petting her. You will do things that may seem a little odd: put your fingers in her ears, play with her toes, squeeze her nose, gently pull her tail, touch her teeth, gums and tongue, touch every part of her face, touch her legs and gently pull them back and forth, give her a back massage, play with her fur, hold her in different positions, roll her onto her back and give her belly rubs! Why? Because for many different reasons, over the course of her life, you are going to have to handle her in these ways. You will have to regularly clean her ears, cut her nails, brush her fur, and brush her teeth. You will have to check her fur for fleas and ticks. You may have to give her eye drops or clean a wound on her skin. You will have to bring her to the vet where she will be poked, prodded, and pulled. You may have to pull her tail to break up a fight. You will certainly have to pull something out of her mouth that she isn't supposed to be chewing on. If you have handled her in the ways we suggest, she is going to be used to it. She might not love having her nails clipped or going to the vet, but she will not be afraid because she trusts you, and she is familiar with the way these weird things feel.

Getting your puppy used to the sensation of a collar and walking on a leash is really an extension of touch and handling. Having on a collar is an unnatural feeling, and being attached to a long rope and having one's movement restricted in this way is really freaky for most pups. Be calm and gentle, and start with the collar in the apartment, then add the leash. In the beginning, she is not going to like it, but trust us, she will get used to it. Don't fall into the trap of not using the leash and collar because your puppy doesn't like it — if you do this, you are only going to make life more uncomfortable for your puppy and yourself in the long run. If your pup pulls on the leash and collar you can use a harness for outside walks until she is old enough to teach not to pull, at about 4 months.

MISSING THE SOCIALIZATION WINDOW

Many dog parents will never have the opportunity to socialize their dog during the critical 7-12 week window for the simple reason that they did not have her yet. If you've adopted an older puppy or an adult dog, she may or may not have been properly socialized as a puppy and it will probably be obvious. If she is balanced and friendly with dogs and people, she was properly socialized. If she is anxious, fearful, or aggressive, unfortunately you cannot turn back the clock — the window for puppy socialization really is definitive. What you can do is move forward with obedience training, for which we offer a step-by-step guide in the next chapter, and incrementally begin to improve social responses and address behavioral problems as they arise.

PUPPY TRAINING: LANGUAGE

Learning language can be a really fun and exciting part of building a relationship with your new puppy, and it is so important. We don't mean you are going to start speaking in barks or that you will teach your puppy a verbal vocabulary of a thousand words. Rather, you and your puppy will become attuned to one another, to body language, to voice, and to routine. Your puppy will show you how she feels, what she needs, and what she wants, and you will begin to understand her. Likewise, you will introduce your puppy to clear body language, a few commands, the nuances of your voice, your routine, and she will begin to respond. When we brought our firstborn daughter home from the hospital, it was magical and beautiful, but also terrifying because we didn't know how to communicate with this little creature. While dog training has not always been a useful background in the rearing of our children, in this it was. Ovidiu approached the new relationship with patience and attunement. He knew that if we paid attention and spent enough time together, we would begin to understand each other and to read the signals from our baby. It is just so with a new puppy.

First, get to know each other. You will be spending a lot of time with your puppy supervising her, giving her affection, and playing with her. Particularly through play, you will be exploring communications with your puppy.

Second, introduce your puppy to three clear messages you will need in your arsenal: praise, displeasure, and neutral communications or commands. We'll guide you through each type of communication, but first it is important to emphasize the principles that apply to whatever kind of language you are using:

Keep your vocabulary minimal, repetitive, and consistent.

By vocabulary we don't just mean words, we mean gestures, body language, and intonations as well. The best way to be clear in communication is to keep it simple and practice a lot.

Don't rely solely on your voice.

Dogs can learn human words, but audio signals are not the main method of communication for dogs. They are much better at using their noses and eyes. Even touch is more important to a dog than sound.

NEUTRAL COMMAND:

This is the voice, body language, and verbal language you are going to use when you ask something of your dog. You won't be doing serious obedience training until your puppy is a bit older, but you will be introducing her to phrases and expressions that you are going to use for the rest of her life. You may not even realize that you are doing it, but you will start to ask things of your dog or tell her to do things like "let's go," and she will be listening.

For this, and later for obedience commands, your voice should be calm, casual, clear, and neutral. You are finding the balance here between making yourself heard and understood, without communicating excitement or displeasure.

 Your Vocabulary: Interdiction. You will need a word to express that you would like your dog to stop doing something, to communicate that she shouldn't do what she is about to do, or to leave something alone. For example, your pup is about to jump in the pond, but you've just given her a bath; or, after twenty minutes of fetch she is still nudging you with the ball and you want to end the game; or, she catches a whiff of fried chicken on the street and starts to wander in that direction. Your tone is neutral because she isn't doing something taboo, it's just something you want her to stop right now. Ovidiu uses the word "fooey." It can be anything that makes sense to you. We hear a lot of people use "leave it," which is fine, but we find a little odd when the "it" is another dog or a person.

PRAISE:

This is the easy one for most dog parents! Figure out how to express to your puppy that you are happy with what she has done. Don't be subtle — with your posture, voice, body language, and words you are going to send the clear message that you are excited and that she is the beneficiary of the excitement. The words you use, like "good girl," will be higher pitched, warm, and elongated. Toys, affection, and treats are also used as rewards to show that you are pleased with something your puppy has done. However, you do not want to distract your puppy for too long from the task at hand or work her up into an over-excited state. Offer the praise, make yourself clear, then return to the play or training.

DISPLEASURE:

Learning to express displeasure to your puppy is the most nuanced and most difficult type of communication for dog parents. You must walk a very fine line of conveying the message to your puppy that you are unhappy and you are in control, without scaring her. You will use a ***firm voice, dominating posture, and short words*** — something like "hey."

For the first few weeks, you will not express displeasure to your puppy at all. You will have created an environment that sets her up for success, and only once she is familiar with the things she is supposed to do, will you give her a bit more space to teach her what she is *not* supposed to do. Even then, the way you express displeasure will be in the absolute most minimal way possible.

PUPPY TRAINING: HOUSETRAINING AND FORMATION OF GOOD HABITS

Obviously knowing where to pee and poop is a priority for most dog parents, but we have paired housetraining with the formation of other good habits because they are linked to the end goal. By the age of around 4-6 months old, we want to have a *well-behaved dog who is free in the apartment or house.* This means that she not only pees outside, but she knows what to chew and what not to chew, she knows what to play with and where to sleep, and she feels comfortable and calm in her home. The habits that you teach your puppy at this stage are largely dependent on your preferences. Do you want a dog who sleeps on the furniture? Do you want a dog who greets people at the door with excitement or remains calm? Keep in mind when making these decisions that your puppy will eventually be an adult dog, and the habits you set now are going to stick. Jumping and chewing might be cute now, but when she is 75 pounds your guests may not think it's very nice!

HOUSETRAINING:

THE BEST APPROACH —

There are three approaches to housetraining. In the first, a puppy is only ever allowed to pee outside, no wee wee pads. While this can be done with dogs who live in the countryside and have uninterrupted access to the outside, it is usually not feasible in the urban environment. Puppies need to pee and poop frequently and as soon as the urge hits, and they should be allowed to do so. There simply is not enough time to get outside.

In the second approach, only wee wee pads are used and a puppy is never taught to pee and poop outside. We think the pitfalls of this approach are self-evident, but just in case, here are a few: reliance on wee wee pads often leads to fewer walks for the doggy who desperately needs them, you'll have a stinky apartment, and you will produce a lifetime of landfill waste.

In the third approach, which is the one we advocate, puppies are taught to use both wee wee pads in the house and to go outside. The pads are gradually reduced in number then entirely removed by the time the puppy has learned the concept and is physically developed enough to pee and poop with less frequency at regular intervals.

THE BIG PICTURE —

In summary, housetraining looks like this: you will place wee wee pads in strategic locations around your house. Every time you see your puppy start to poop or pee, you will place her on the nearest wee wee pad. At the same time, she will get regular walks and be praised for peeing and pooping outside. Gradually, as she learns where to pee, you will remove the less frequently used wee wee pads until there is only one left. She will eventually only want to go outside, and when this happens you will get rid of the last wee wee pad, and your puppy is housetrained.

Sounds easy, right? Well, it isn't rocket science, but housetraining does depend on dedication and vigilance, and the devil is often in the details. So here they are:

Pen.

When you bring home your puppy at around 8 weeks old, you will need to have a space prepared for her where she will stay when she is not being supervised. We recommend having a pen

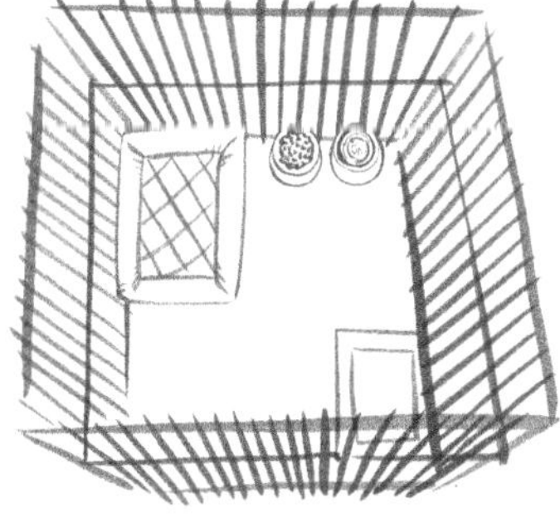

with enough space for a wee wee pad, a bed, toys, food, water, and maybe a crate. The size of the space will depend on the size of your puppy but should roughly be 5 feet by 5 feet at a minimum. The wee wee pad should be at the opposite side from bed and food. For the first few weeks or months, this is where your puppy will be at night when everyone is sleeping, when she is alone during the day, and if someone is home but cannot be supervising.

Crate.

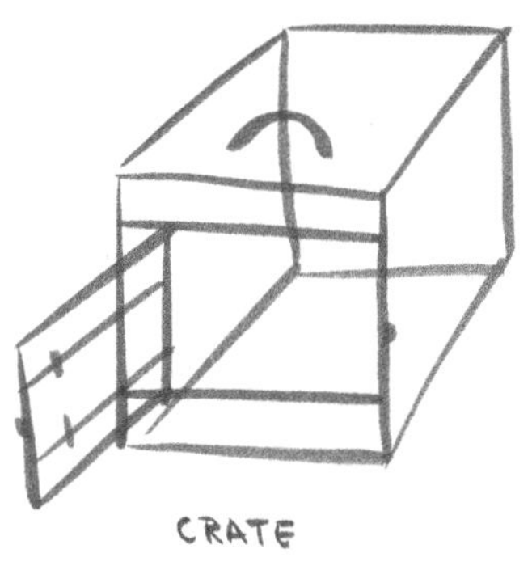

CRATE

We don't use crates for housetraining. Many people do because they are the greatest natural inhibitor of accidents: it goes against a puppy's instinct to pee or poop where she sleeps. This might sound very useful, but for puppies we think it is a bad choice. Puppies need to pee a lot. It is normal and natural. If your puppy is crated for a long period of time you will either force her to pee on her bed or force her to be uncomfortable while she holds it. Housetraining isn't about preventing your puppy from peeing, it is about teaching her where the proper place to pee is, and we think that crating a puppy is setting her up for failure, not for success. A small pen will achieve the same goal of limiting the floorspace for an accident, while still providing your puppy with a clean place to sleep and continuous access to a permissible place to pee. Having an open crate inside the pen with a bed inside is fine and is a good way to get your dog used to a crate, which you may have to use in the future for travel.

Wee Wee Pads.

You will have wee wee pads strategically placed around your home, and the number of pads should correspond to the size of the space that your puppy has supervised

access to. Strategically placed means that it is always easy for your puppy to get to one when she has to go, and if she is having an accident, there is always one close by for you to place her on. Keep the location of the pads consistent so that as your puppy learns to use them, she will also know where they are.

Cleaning Supplies.

Be sure to have odor-eliminating cleaning supplies on hand. Throughout the housetraining process it is important to clean accidents immediately and thoroughly. If your pup smells pee on the floor it will remind her that maybe it was a good spot to pee, and she will do it again, quickly forming a habit.

Supervising and Vigilance.

Supervising your puppy means watching her with 100% vigilance. As soon as she starts to poop or pee, not a minute or even a few seconds later, you will pick her up and place her on the nearest wee wee pad. You will not be reading a book, watching television, or sending emails. Why? Because this is an absolutely critical time when your puppy is learning the rules of her new home, and if she is allowed to pee on the floor (i.e., nobody stopped her from doing it), it will become a habit that is very hard to break. Do you have to supervise her all of the time? Of course not, that is why you have set up a comfortable space for her to sleep, eat, drink, pee, and poop when you cannot be watching her with vigilance.

Food and Water.

As soon as possible, you will get your puppy on an eating schedule. Puppies need to eat at least 3 times per day, and water should always be available. Young puppies have tiny bladders and need to pee frequently, but you should start to see pooping patterns almost immediately. Make sure you are walking your puppy outside at the times she usually needs to poop; for most puppies this is after eating. Eventually you will also see patterns for peeing because your puppy will drink more water at specific times — with meals and after exercising.

Schedule.

In the beginning weeks, your puppy should not be left alone for more than a couple of hours at a time. As she gets older this period can extend to 3-4 hours.

STAGE 1 HOUSETRAINING —

In the beginning, assume your puppy doesn't know anything about where to poop and pee. Assume that she is going to have accidents. In this first stage, you will be gently introducing her to the concept of where to pee and poop in two ways:

1) by placing her on the wee wee pad as soon as you see her start to pee or poop, and
2) by rewarding her when she goes on her own to the proper place to pee or poop.

At this first stage of learning, it is very important to note that you will not be communicating displeasure to your puppy for peeing or pooping on the floor. She doesn't know the rules yet. She will learn them, but right now it is your job to be calm, patient, and vigilant. When she starts to go on the floor, immediately lift her up and place her on a wee wee pad. Do this quickly and calmly. (The goal here is to be as unintrusive as possible so that she is not startled. We don't want puppy to feel uncomfortable peeing in front of you — it may make her inclined to hide when she pees). After you have calmly picked her up and moved her, she may finish on the wee wee pad. This is wonderful, but it is not the time to offer praise.

You will offer praise and treats when you see your puppy pee or poop in the proper place *on her own* (you have not placed her on the wee wee pad). Whether she voluntarily walks to the wee wee pad in the house or you are walking her outside, ***as soon as she is finished pooping or peeing***, make your happiness obvious, tell her what a good girl she is, and give her a treat. It is important to note here that timing is critical. You cannot show excitement or offer praise while she is still peeing because she will either stop without finishing or start running to you and tinkle along the way. Be patient, but also be ready. The praise must come as soon as she is finished if she is to know what she is being praised for. It may seem obvious, but this also means that if you find pee on a wee wee pad, but you didn't see her do it (even if it has only been a few minutes!) it is too late to reward her. Wait until the next time.

STAGE 2 HOUSETRAINING —

The next stage of housetraining is to begin eliminating wee wee pads with the goal of getting down to just one. This process begins as soon as your puppy demonstrates that she is learning the concept of where to pee and poop. In as little as a few days or up to a few weeks, your puppy will start going to the wee wee pad on her own, most of the time. She will also be holding it a little longer, and you may begin to see patterns of timing develop. Begin removing wee wee pads one at a time and be strategic in your choice. If there is one pad she never uses, toss it. Leave those that she uses more frequently. If you remove a wee wee pad and she starts having a lot of accidents, you may have moved too quickly. Put it back, then try again in a few days or whenever she is ready.

Throughout all of this time your puppy will be getting lots of walks outside as well. This is incredibly important for all sorts of reasons, but with respect to housetraining, walks allow your puppy's natural instinct to pee outside to develop. All dogs like relieving themselves in a natural environment, and eventually your puppy will prefer it as well. It is also critical that your walks start happening on a regular schedule and that they are timed in coordination with when your puppy usually needs to pee and poop, like after eating. Gradually, patterns will form.

At this point, your puppy knows she should go on a wee wee pad or outside, and while you are still rewarding her with praise and treats for going in the proper place, this is the time that you can begin associating accidents with something unpleasant. She understands the concept (we know this because she gets it right at least 85% of the time), so it is now appropriate to make her slightly uncomfortable when she pees on the floor. Instead of gently picking her up and moving her to the pad when she starts peeing, you will lift her in a way that is awkward but not painful by holding the scruff or by applying a gentle pressure under her arms where you hold her and tilting her slightly to one side as you carry her to the wee wee pad. You will not express displeasure at this point, because you run the risk that your puppy thinks the act of peeing displeases you, not understanding that the problem is merely where she pees. By simply picking her up and moving her in a way that is a little bit unpleasant, she will begin to prefer peeing on the wee wee pad every time. If she finishes peeing on the pad after you have moved her, do not offer praise (remember, praise is only for when she voluntarily walks to the pad or goes outside).

PUPPY BEING LIFTED
AT A TILT

PUPPY BEING LIFTED
BY SCRUFF

STAGE 3 HOUSETRAINING —

You are almost there! Your puppy could be anywhere from about 3 to 5 months at this point. You have one wee wee pad left in your house, probably by the front door, but most of the time your puppy is peeing and pooping outside. You have also established a feeding and walking schedule for your pup that is aligned with her need for relieving herself. She will be eating three times a day and have a minimum of four walks. At some point, your puppy will almost entirely stop using the wee wee pad because she prefers to go outside. When this happens, get rid of the last wee wee pad and, congratulations, you have a housetrained puppy!

SETBACKS AND PROBLEMS —

Sometimes puppies seem to be learning the rules, but after removing one or more wee wee pads they have more accidents. If this regression happens, it may mean that you moved a little bit too fast, and you will have to take one step back. You will reintroduce a wee wee pad where your puppy is having accidents. Make sure that your puppy is in her pen when unsupervised and remember to supervise her with the same high level of vigilance when she is free in the house as when you started the process.

Also be sure your pup is getting enough outdoor exercise. We often see dogs regress or have accidents when they aren't going for regular, rigorous walks. Remember how key this is to the training and overall wellbeing of your pup.

If your ***fully trained puppy starts having accidents,*** it could also be a sign of something more serious like physical illness. Urinary tract infections are a common culprit, but there are many, many types of physical problems, illnesses, foods, even medications that can make your dog have to urinate with more frequency, that can make her less able to hold it, or that can cause diarrhea. Never hesitate to schedule a visit to your veterinarian if you notice a sudden change. In some cases, a simple shift in diet can be the fix, in other cases it is more serious.

If your puppy is ***chewing up the wee wee pads,*** there are a few ways to fix the problem. First, this should never be happening when she is out of the pen — remember, if she is out of the pen she is supervised, and you will treat chewing the wee wee pad like any other inappropriate chewing. This is addressed in the next section. However, if she is chewing up the pads in her pen when unsupervised the first step is to make sure there is something better in the pen that she is allowed to chew on, like some toys. If this doesn't deter her, the next option is to fix the pad to the floor. There are trays made specifically for this purpose which can be quite effective, or the pad can be taped down.

Once your puppy knows how to use wee wee pads and go outside, you are well on your way to getting rid of the pen altogether. However, she must be able to safely have free reign in your home without supervision, and this means knowing all the house rules.

HOUSE RULES AND THE FORMATION OF GOOD HABITS:

Throughout the process of housetraining your puppy, you will also be teaching her very important house rules and life skills. House rules and life skills or "good habits" are paired together because in order to effectively teach your puppy what she is not allowed to do (chew your shoes), you must concurrently teach her what she is allowed to do (chew the dog toy). She will learn to be comfortable alone, she will learn to not jump or whine, and, most importantly, she will learn how to play. You are getting ready to give her free reign in the house, and you are establishing the foundations of balanced behavior.

SAFETY:

Despite the fact that when your puppy is free in your home you will be supervising her, it is critical that you make your home safe. This means putting cables, cleaning supplies, anything toxic, and anything life-threatening out of reach. No matter how vigilant you are, your attention will sometimes lapse when your puppy is not in her pen. Be prepared by removing anything dangerous from your puppy's environment.

WHAT TO CHEW:

Puppies explore the world with their mouths, and when they are bored, they chew. Your new puppy is going to chew things, and it is your job to teach her what is and what is not appropriate to put in her mouth. You will do this in the obvious ways, by giving her things she is allowed to chew and by taking things away that she isn't, and we will take you through that step-by-step process here. But you will also address chewing by engaging your puppy in play, which is a layered concept.

Step 1 Chewing —

You will be guiding your puppy from day one, and the process should be parallel to housetraining. The principle is the same: the pen or safe area you have created for your puppy to stay in when she is unsupervised sets her up for success because she only has access to toys she is allowed to chew. We suggest using toys that cannot be shredded or destroyed; rubber balls are a good choice. If given things like stuffed animals that can be easily unstuffed you will establish a habit that can become problematic. Your puppy will be more inclined to unstuff other things, like furniture and kids' toys.

In the very beginning, you will remove distractions and anything inappropriate and tempting for your puppy to chew from everywhere in your home that your puppy will have access to (not just the pen). You will be supervising her, yes, but at this early stage the first thing you are going to do is play with your puppy and give her appropriate toys to chew on. By removing things like shoes and newspapers, you can teach your puppy to chew on and play with toys in a purely positive manner. When she does find something like the corner of the rug, redirect her attention to play with a toy.

Step 2 Chewing —

After a couple of weeks, you and your puppy will find a good rhythm, you will start to speak the same language, and your puppy is becoming familiar with her toys and play. At this point, you will start to slowly place things into her supervised environment that she is not allowed to chew. When she chooses to go for the shoes or the newspaper, you will introduce the gentlest possible communication of displeasure. It has to be immediate, and may be nothing more than a short, firm, "hey," but if she does not react to your voice alone, you can pair the sound with tough posturing and something slightly uncomfortable. The discomfort should be linked to the unwanted chewing. For example: if your puppy is chewing your hand, press on the back of her tongue with your finger until she pulls away; if she is chewing on the sofa, you can give her a quick, firm, nudge on the chest to signal that she should stop; or, you can lift her by the scruff or collar so that only her back legs are on the floor and gently move her away; a tap on the nose is another useful way to communicate to your pup.

Remember, right now your puppy doesn't necessarily understand what you expect from her when you express displeasure with your voice and posture alone. Adding something slightly uncomfortable is an important way to teach her your language. Immediately after, redirect her to a toy and engage in positive play.

Once your puppy begins to understand your language, when she responds well to your communications of praise and displeasure, and when she is familiar with the toys she is allowed to chew that have been introduced through positive reinforcement, you will challenge her more directly. You will provide easy access to things she isn't allowed to chew, and let her make choices. If she makes the wrong choice you will express your displeasure, and a few minutes later you will give her another opportunity to misbehave. An important part of teaching a puppy your language and the rules is repetition. If she chooses well, she is praised, if she chooses the wrong thing to chew, you repeat the process.

During this period your puppy is still supervised at all times when she is not in her pen or safe space. This process works in tandem with housetraining. As she becomes better and better at knowing what she can and cannot chew, she will have more freedom in your home.

Step 3 Chewing —

Ideally, when you remove the safe zone you have created for your puppy — the pen — she will be well behaved and you won't need to "puppy-proof" anything (like shoes). But be smart and realistic. Keep anything dangerous tucked away. Your puppy is still learning, and while the goal is to eventually have an adult dog who behaves as well when home alone as she does when in your presence, she probably isn't there yet. Remain vigilant and consistent, and most importantly, engage her in plenty of positive play!

HOW TO PLAY:

Teaching your puppy how to play is more important and more involved than most readers expect. Play isn't just about fun and exercise: it is a way of interacting with your puppy that will help you ***build a positive relationship*** together; you will learn to ***understand each other;*** you will ***develop skills and habits to promote lifelong learning***; and, it is through play that you will ***introduce motivating factors and the concept of obedience training***.

Play requires work and engagement from you — it is your job to keep your puppy's attention by showing excitement and by rewarding her when she plays well, and the rewards should be more than treats. This is your opportunity to introduce a variety of motivating factors to your puppy: affection, praise, treats, and play itself. It might seem like a good idea to give your puppy destructible toys that she can chew up and play independently with, but we caution against this. Pick toys that cannot be destroyed because we want to encourage play, not destruction. Does this require more engagement from you? Absolutely, but as with everything related to puppy training, the work will pay off because you will have a well-behaved adult dog.

The key to guiding your puppy in play is to incorporate fun activities that will help later in life and that will facilitate the introduction of obedience training. We'll provide some examples to get you started.

Chase and Retrieve:

The simple act of throwing a ball or toy for your puppy and teaching her how to bring it back to you is one of the most useful skills she will learn. If your puppy can chase and retrieve, you have an invaluable, lifelong tool for exercise and stimulation that can be adapted to any environment — inside or outside, city or country. In addition, the game sets the groundwork for teaching your puppy how to "come." Before you throw the ball for your puppy, make sure she is paying attention to it. Show it to her and say "ready?!" Make sure she is watching where you throw the ball, and when she picks it up immediately praise her and encourage her to bring it back while moving away. By moving backwards, away from your pup, you are actually incentivizing her to come to you. Her instinct to follow kicks in. Reward her with praise and affection when she brings it back. Then repeat.

An enhanced version of chase and retrieve is to use two balls. As soon as your puppy returns with the first ball, she will see that you have a second ball in your hand. This will encourage her to immediately drop the ball she has just retrieved, and as she does so you will reward her by throwing the second ball, and the game continues this way.

Tug o' War:

Some readers will see tug o' war and ask, "Won't that make my puppy aggressive?" Absolutely not. That is a widespread but completely false myth. Tug o' war is fun; it is a great game for bonding with your puppy; and it helps her build her strength.

Running:

Running with your puppy does not mean putting her on a leash and jogging around a track while you listen to music. This is a different kind of running. Leashed or off leash, you are going to run while keeping her engaged. Start off running backwards and enticing her to follow you. It is a game. As she catches on make it more difficult by stopping, turning, darting from side to side. She will be excited as long as you are paying attention to her and interacting. Again, this activity is great for bonding and exercise, but will also lay the foundations for teaching her to come because your puppy will learn that running to you is fun.

For more games, like hide and seek, refer back to the Exercise and Activities chapter.

JUMPING, EXCITEMENT AND WHINING:

Some people love it when they walk in the door and their dog starts whining, barking, jumping and showing other signs of excitement. It might be cute when your 10-pound puppy jumps on your leg to greet you, but remember our story about Zuzu? It's not so cute when she is bigger and older and you end up having to put her in a room by herself so she doesn't knock over the kids who are visiting.

Your puppy will mirror you, so the first step in teaching your puppy how to stay calm and relaxed is to model these behaviors. When you come home you should be quiet and disinterested in your puppy. If your puppy jumps, make her mildly uncomfortable by pushing your leg outward. This will put her slightly off balance, and she will stop. Put away the groceries and give your puppy a few minutes to relax before greeting her with a calm voice and affection.

In general, whining for attention should be ignored, not rewarded. You will give your puppy affection when you are ready and when she is in a relaxed state. Remember, you are setting the boundaries now for a lifetime together.

SEPARATION:

As soon as you bring your puppy home, you will need to start "practicing" alone time. It can be difficult to leave your itty-bitty furball, especially if she whines and cries in your absence, but do not let that deter you. The principle, or goal, is to teach your puppy that being alone is not scary but comfortable. It is a time to rest and relax. If you miss the early window to teach your puppy this lesson, you run the risk of having an adult dog with separation anxiety, and this is an extremely difficult situation for parent and dog.

The best way to help your puppy learn to have a relaxed state of mind when left alone is to set her up for success by exercising her vigorously before leaving. Feed your puppy then take her for a long walk outside. Play with her on the walk, directly engaging her. The first time you leave her should be just after you bring home an exhausted puppy. Her instinct to curl up and sleep will be stronger than her instinct to miss you, and soon after she wakes up from her long nap you will come home to greet her. You are helping your puppy establish positive associations with alone time from a very young age.

WALKING ON A LEASH:

Until your puppy is about 5 to 6 months old and ready for obedience training, you are only going to be getting her used to the idea of walking with both a collar and a harness. You will not yet be teaching her to heel or introducing corrections for pulling, but if she bites the leash you will stop her by saying a firm "hey" and removing the leash from her mouth if she doesn't drop it. Take her for regular walks with different kinds of collars and harnesses. Harnesses should always be attached to the leash from the back, not the chest. Harnesses attached to the chest are designed to prevent pulling by inhibiting your dog's natural movement, which should not be your goal (we discuss this in more detail in the Gear chapter). Rather, if your puppy is a heavy puller, a harness will be the best choice for everyday walks until she is old enough for obedience training. In effect, you are allowing her to pull until you can properly teach her not to, and pulling with a collar is not safe. Even if you usually opt for a harness instead of a collar at this point, make sure you are still getting her used to the collar because when she is a bit older, this will be the best choice for everyday walks.

If your puppy plants her feet in the ground and doesn't walk once leashed, these early months are an ideal time to encourage her to walk by offering play, affection, and treats. Rainy days are often the biggest challenge, but the principle is the same. Make sure she knows that walks are fun. It is your job to keep her happy and interested.

SETBACKS AND ADOLESCENCE:

For the first six months to one year of your puppy's life, you will likely see predictable progress with training and generally good behavior, with some minor setbacks. However, at around one year, your puppy will reach adolescence, and you will be scratching your head wondering what the heck went wrong. Don't fret; it is perfectly normal. Your pup is now a cool and confident teenager, and she is going to push the boundaries and challenge you. You will remain consistent, never letting your trouble-making teen win the battle. It will pass.

STAY
READY?!

CHAPTER 10

OBEDIENCE TRAINING

WHAT IS OBEDIENCE TRAINING?

Obedience training is what most people think of when they hear the word "training." It involves teaching your dog to respond with a specific act or set of actions when she is given a command, like "come." We don't start obedience training until puppies are about 6 months old, but dogs at any age can learn new commands. What obedience doesn't include is tracking, protection, agility, and other specialized training.[11]

OBEDIENCE TRAINING FOR AN URBAN DOG is essential for the obvious reason: keeping your pup under control in the crowded, chaotic, and sometimes dangerous environs of the city requires that your pup respond to basic commands like "come," "sit," and "stay." However, it is also critical because through obedience training you will learn to communicate more effectively with your dog and to establish a set of

---

11)   Some training methods, like Schutzhund, which originated with training dogs for police work, include obedience, tracking, and protection as one comprehensive approach. Such specialized training is not covered in this book.

norms and expectations. Your dog will learn to dependably listen to commands until given a release command. In addition, when you are displeased with your dog, you will know how to properly express yourself, and she will know what is expected of her. A dog who is practiced will back out of the fight at the dog park when Mom says "hey" or stop chasing the squirrel into the street. ***Through obedience training you will build an understanding and a toolkit not only for teaching your pup new commands but for keeping her safe.***

We'll take you through a step-by-step example of training a dog to "come" and "sit-stay" followed by tips on how to teach your dog to walk on a leash. The tools through these examples can be applied to teaching your dog any number of commands and tricks.

While tricks aren't essential in the sense of being necessary to keep your dog safe and under control, they can be very useful in other ways. Teaching your dog new things is really fun and stimulating for her and will help you to build a positive relationship together. In fact, if you do it properly, your dog will love obedience training!

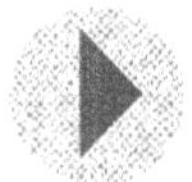

After reading this chapter, we strongly urge you to make use of our training videos available on our YouTube channel: www.youtube.com/user/NycDoggies.

It is difficult, if not impossible, to really learn how to train a dog without actually watching someone do it and then practicing yourself. We do our best to put the process into words, but we think most readers will get maximum value from this section by first reading, then watching videos while practicing.

THE PROCESS IN A NUTSHELL:

Obedience training is a three-part process. We use the terms Teaching, Proofing, and Maintenance to describe the three stages because they best describe the principles involved. All new commands are introduced in the teaching phase using positive reinforcement. Once the concept of the command has been learned, it is "proofed" or tested in different environments and with more distractions until your dog has mastered the command and reliably responds. In the proofing phase, obedience is rewarded and disobedience triggers enforcement. After that, regular practice — ideally daily — is important for maintaining obedience.

LANGUAGE AND EFFECTIVE COMMUNICATION:

If you are just jumping into the book at this point because you need guidance on how to train an adult dog, we recommend reading both the Foundations of Training and the Language section in the Puppy Training chapter before you begin.

In order to train your dog, no matter the age, breed, or personality, you will first have to establish effective communication. We'll review the main points here.

1) You need to have a ***relationship*** with the dog you are training. Presumably you are training your own dog, and you understand each other well. You know how to engage your dog in play, and you can read each other's body language.

2) You know what ***motivates*** your dog. Is she driven by food? Toys? Affection? Is she sensitive to your voice when you are displeased?

3) You have practiced and can effectively ***communicate*** with words, tone, and body language three things to your dog: ***Praise, Neutral Commands, Displeasure***.

PRAISE:

The easiest type of communication for most people, praise is all about expressing how happy you are with whatever your pup has just done. You will use elongated words, a lighter tone, and relaxed body language to say things like, "Good girl!"

NEUTRAL COMMANDS:

When you ask your dog to do something, you must be clear, calm, and confident. You are finding a balance between making sure you are heard and understood, without communicating excitement or displeasure.

OBEDIENCE COMMANDS — commands like "come," "sit," and "stay," will be paired with a clear hand gesture.

INTERDICTION — this is a word like "fooey" or "leave it" that expresses your desire for your dog to stop doing something, without expressing displeasure. For example, your dog pushes her ball to your feet, but the game of chase is over, so you say "fooey" and she stops.

RELEASE — this is a word or phrase like "okay, go!" that tells your dog she is released from whatever command she was obeying, such as "sit-stay."

DISPLEASURE:

You will use a short word like "hey" that immediately gets your dog's attention from within a few feet to long distances. What you are trying to achieve by saying "hey" (or whatever word you choose) is this: as soon as your pup hears the word from you, she will stop whatever she is doing, knowing that you disapprove of the action, then give her attention to you.

You will need to say the word in a *deep* but *loud* voice that carries from wherever you are standing to wherever your dog is. It must be a word that cannot be misinterpreted by your dog because it is only used when you need to communicate with her sharply and effectively. The word and tone are paired with tough body language; essentially, you will puff yourself up and appear dominating.

POSITIVE TRAINING AND ENFORCEMENT:

In general, training should be a happy experience for both

you and your dog. Wherever and whenever possible, we use a positive approach — this means positive stimuli and rewards are used to motivate a dog to learn a specific command or behavior. It is effective, fun, and helps cultivate a strong relationship between dog and parent. It is also a science-based approach; obedience training is about teaching dogs to *do* something, to *act*, to obey a command. As it happens, animals and humans alike respond well to positive reinforcement for learning to *take some sort of action,* i.e., obedience training.[12] However, there are times in obedience training when, with most dogs, it is necessary for Mom or Dad to communicate displeasure and to enforce a command. Thus, for obedience training we use a system of positive encouragement and rewards paired with **enforcement.**

WHAT IS IT?

All new concepts are taught with positive training in the teaching phase. As distractions are added in the proofing phase there may be times when rewards and encouragement are not enough to entice your dog to action, and in these situations you will use enforcement. This means demanding obedience by

1) getting your dog's full attention by communicating displeasure and

2) enforcing the command through physical manipulation.

---

12) On the flip side, negative stimuli (what trainers call "corrections") are more effective for stopping unwanted behaviors ranging from chewing socks to aggression.

With an enforcement you are teaching your dog that disobedience isn't an option. For example, Luna hears you say "come" but she chooses to wander in the other direction. In brief, if you are holding the leash you will get her attention by snapping the leash and saying "hey" in a displeased voice, then you will enforce the command by quickly walking her by the leash to the exact spot at which you were standing when you asked her to come.

WHY ENFORCEMENT?

In most cases, it is impossible to guarantee dependent responses to commands without some form of enforcement. Why? Because in order to expect obedience based purely on a reward, the reward always has to be the most attractive, most motivating factor to your dog in a given situation. As skills are practiced in different environments with more and more distractions during proofing, this becomes more and more difficult to achieve. Going for a hike or an off-leash walk in the city park is often the ultimate test for a dog's responsiveness because the distractions are everywhere, they are exciting, and they are accessible. We've faced this issue with pups who have been trained in specific environments, but when they join us for hikes they are faced with a whole new world of exciting distractions.

On Jen's first hike with Maggie, a generally responsive, mixed-breed shepherd, a showdown ensued when Maggie treed a raccoon. Normally a food and affection driven pup, nothing — not even beef jerky — could convince Maggie that "coming" was a good option. Why would she come when the alternative, barking at a real, live animal, was so much fun? Jen tugged her collar and demanded Maggie's attention with a firm voice before quickly leading her back to the place Jen was standing when she initially asked Maggie to come. That was enough. Once Maggie learned that Jen was going to require her to "come" no matter what fun distractions the forest offered up, she listened.

Another pup, however, had to quit the hikes because he did not have a dependent "come," and his family opted for a positive reinforcement-only approach, which we respected. Hugo was a one-hundred-pound, unfixed Rhodesian ridgeback with a sweet personality and a penchant for the lady dogs. Hugo was driven by affection, and at home in the city he would do anything for a pat or a snuggle. But on the trails, one tiny whiff of a female dog and he was off to the races. Nothing we could offer was enough of an incentive to keep him close. In order to continue hiking his trainer would have to work on some important commands, but the family insisted he was perfectly obedient, and the trainer was opposed to introducing any enforcement. Unfortunately, we had to discontinue hikes for Hugo.

No matter how obedient you think your pup is, there will probably come a day when you discover the raccoon — or the garbage, or the neighbor's dog in heat — and all of a sudden whatever you have to offer is not enough. In this sense, dogs are very rational and deserve some intellectual credit. Why go for the tennis ball when there is an actual cat running across the street? What enforcement achieves, is to make the cat less attractive because you have taught your pup that no matter what she tries, you will not accept disobedience. And this lesson might very well save her life one day.

We think it is only fair that if we expect dogs to respond to what we ask, then we have to make those expectations clear. By using positive reinforcement to teach new skills, and then a combination of positive rewards and enforcement during the proofing phase of training, you can establish clear guidelines and clear expectations for your pup.

HOW TO ENFORCE?

Once your dog has learned a new command, you will move on to the proofing phase of obedience training. As difficulty is increased by adding more distractions in proofing, you will likely be met with disobedience at some point. Disobedience triggers the 3-step enforcement process:

1) communication of displeasure,
2) physically enforcing obedience, and
3) practicing the command.

However, over time you will stop needing to use step 2 because your dog will learn what your communication of displeasure means. The more consistent you are, the easier it will be for your pup to learn the rules. She will obey if she expects enforcement because you have been consistent, every single time.

STEP 1: COMMUNICATE DISPLEASURE
TO GET FULL ATTENTION —

The moment your dog disobeys, you will indicate that you are unhappy. The goal is to get her full attention as quickly as possible. You will say "hey" in a loud, firm voice with tough body language. The intensity of your communication will depend on a number of factors. How big is the distraction or temptation? Is your pup strong-willed? Is she wearing a leash? If she is wearing a leash, you have a great tool for strengthening your communication to her by giving it a quick snap.

 Snap the leash. A leash snap is one of the most effective ways to get your dog's attention quickly, but it must be done properly. The leash must be slack in order to send a quick snap to the collar. If the behavior occurs when the leash is taught, create some slackness by briefly releasing the tension — move your hand closer to your dog if need be. A proper snap is created by a flick movement of the hand which sends an arc down the length of the leash to the dog's neck. If you cannot master the snap, a quick tug is also effective. Just be sure to relieve the tension immediately. A taught leash that is pulled on will only have the effect of encouraging your dog to pull harder.

With practice, as soon as your dog hears your communication of displeasure, her response will be to give you her full and immediate attention while performing the command you initially gave her. When this happens, you will skip to step 3. Physical enforcement becomes unnecessary. However, in the beginning you will probably not get obedience with just a vocal "hey" because your pup does not yet know what the process is and what to expect. Once you have her attention you will move on to the next step, enforcing obedience.

STEP 2: ENFORCE OBEDIENCE —

You have your pup's attention, she knows you are displeased, now it is time to show her exactly what you expect. You will do this by physically moving your dog. If she didn't come when she was called, you will take her by the leash (putting one on if she isn't on a leash) and walk her to the place at which you were standing when you first called "come." If she didn't sit, you will hold her by the collar with one hand and apply a gentle pressure to her rear with the other until she sits. If she didn't stay, you will walk her to the place she was sitting when you asked her to stay and so on.

The idea is simple, but execution is often not. The problem parents run into when trying to enforce a command is that the dog begins to walk or run away. There are two ways to avoid this challenge. ***First, make sure your initial communication is strong enough.*** If your pup knows you are serious, she is less likely to bounce away. Of course, freshly trained pups will often run away even if they know you are serious because they have not yet learned the process. This can be mitigated with our second suggestion, ***attach a long lead to your pup.*** She will be less likely to run away because she feels the weight of the lead, and if she runs, she will be easier to catch. And catch her you must. Whether it takes 10 seconds or 40 minutes, if your pup runs away after receiving your initial communication of displeasure, you must catch her and follow through with enforcing obedience to the initial command. With this kind of consistency, your dog will learn that disobedience is never an option, and running away will no longer cross her mind.

STEP 3: PRACTICE THE COMMAND —

After you have physically enforced the initial command, you will immediately practice the command again. Whether you are proofing a new distraction or environment or maintaining the skills of a trained dog, it is important to resume training practice after any enforcement. If your dog doesn't understand by the second or third try that she must obey, you have either

1) moved to fast in adding more challenging distractions or
2) not communicated effectively.

Throughout training, including when you are using enforcement, you will be giving your dog plenty of short breaks and watching carefully for signs of fatigue and stress. Finally, don't hold a grudge. Enforcement is brief, and when it's over, it's over.

GUIDE TO TRAINING: "COME," "SIT-STAY"

WE HAVE SAID IT before and we will say it again here — every dog is different, which will translate into a slightly different training experience for each and every dog parent. It is impossible to offer a one-size-fits-all training manual that can be applied without modification and nuance. Instead, what we will do here is to take you through the training steps with the example of one dog, Fred.

It is the responsibility of every reader to adapt these lessons to the specific personality of your pup and to the environment you have access to for training. We hope we have given you the tools to do so.

PREPARATIONS:

WHO: Fred is a medium sized, mixed-breed puppy — probably part shepherd and part retriever. He is six months old, healthy, full of energy, and has been well socialized throughout puppyhood. Fred knows and responds to his name, and he and Ovidiu have gotten to know each other well. Ovidiu easily engages Fred in play and knows his preferences for hot dogs and rubber balls. Fred gives his attention to Ovidiu when asked, and they are able to clearly communicate with each other. When Ovidiu walks to the refrigerator for some treats and then the closet for a leash, Fred knows that this is his cue to get ready for a walk.

WHAT: Fred is going to learn to come, to sit, and to stay in daily one-hour training sessions, each followed by multiple 5-10-minute practice sessions throughout the day. The "stay" command is introduced only once Fred understands the concept of "sit" and begins doing so on command, and eventually the "sit" and "stay" commands will be linked so that when Fred sits, he automatically expects to stay until given a release command. Some dogs will learn the concept of the three commands in one or two days and spend the next week proofing; for others, the teaching phase will take longer.

WHERE: Training sessions will begin in a quiet, outdoor space, free from distractions.

TEACHING PHASE:

On his first day of training, Ovidiu and Fred wake up bright and early and, before breakfast, head to a quiet corner of the local park.

 *Training sessions are always scheduled in the morning when dogs are full of energy, thus more engaged, alert, and better able to absorb the information they are learning. Breakfast will be the treats that are given as rewards during the training session.*

Ovidiu has a pouch attached to his belt with high-reward treats, in this case sliced up hot dogs, and a bag with Fred's favorite rubber balls. Fred is excited for his walk and for a fun outing to the park.

 Training sessions should always be a fun activity for pups; this is how their attention, engagement, and motivation are maintained.

Ovidiu walks Fred on a standard 6-foot leash to the park, but once they reach the quiet corner where the lesson will take place, Ovidiu switches the leash to a lightweight, 20-foot lead. Ovidiu needs to maintain control of Fred, who cannot yet be trusted off leash. At the same time, he must give Fred freedom and space during the lesson. The long lead achieves this balance.

Ovidiu and Fred find a quiet corner of the park with a

fence on one side and a line of trees that creates a natural border on another side. There are a few people sitting on benches but no other dogs in the immediate area. Fred is energetic and alert, with eyes only for Ovidiu because he has been here before and knows that he is in for a fun-filled morning.

TEACHING STAGE 1:
INTRODUCE THE ACTION AND ASSOCIATE THE ACTION WITH VERBAL COMMAND, A GESTURE, AND A REWARD

In a Nutshell —

In this comfortable and simple environment, you will use play to introduce the desired actions of coming and sitting. As soon as your dog begins to perform the actions, you will say "sit" or "come;" you will pair your words with a hand gesture; and you will offer a reward when the action is completed.

The Process —

Ovidiu begins playing with Fred, and because Ovidiu is the most interesting thing around, he has Fred's full attention. Ovidiu decides not to hold the leash with Fred but to let it drag on the ground. Fred is attentive, not aloof, and it is obvious to Ovidiu that Fred is more interested in him than in chasing anything else in the park. The weight of the leash signals to Fred that he is not completely free, but he has space to run and learn. If he needs to, Ovidiu can pick up or step on the leash to communicate with Fred or to stop him from running away.

Through play, Ovidiu entices Fred to move in all sorts of ways — to run when chasing a ball, to dart from side to side, to jump up, turn around, and of course, to sit and come. Here is how: Ovidiu is holding Fred's favorite ball; he runs backwards (having made sure the path behind him is clear); and he does not lose his focus on Fred.

Fred's instinct will be to follow Ovidiu, and as he begins moving Ovidiu says "come." (If Fred was not fully focused, Ovidiu would have called his name first, then after a brief pause, given the command. The name gets the dog's attention before asking him what to do. If your dog is fully attentive, it is not necessary to call the name first). The verbal command is paired with a gesture. Ovidiu taps his chest with his hand while moving away from Fred.

As Fred moves towards Ovidiu he is given praise: "Good boy, Fred," and once he reaches Ovidiu the praise is exaggerated: "Good boy Fred! Good boy!" The ball is immediately thrown for Fred to retrieve as a reward. Training is a game, and Fred is loving it. After a little while of running to Ovidiu and retrieving the ball, Ovidiu introduces the action of sitting. Ovidiu runs backward with treat in hand and calls Fred. This time when Fred gets to Ovidiu, he slowly lifts the treat over Fred's head while saying "sit."

Fred of course follows the treat with his nose and eyes until his neck starts to bend backwards. At this point, it is natural for any dog to sit because the position becomes more comfortable, and Fred does. When Fred's tush hits the ground and he is fully in the sit position, Ovidiu immediately says "good boy" in a calm and positive voice, using elongated words, and releases the treat as a reward. Next time, Ovidiu uses a ball instead of a treat, to the same result.

 Every command, if possible, should have both a verbal and hand sign. Dogs respond better to hand signs, but when, eventually, there is distance between you and your pup, you will also need a voice command, thus both are introduced from the start.

For "sit," the hand gesture should look something like this:

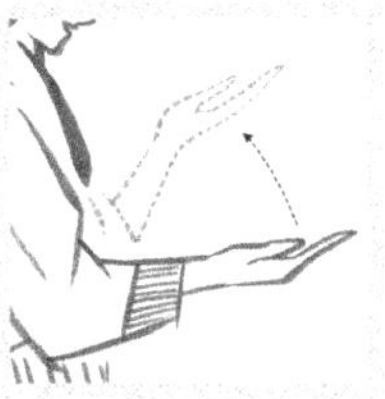

your hand will be raised above the dog's head because the dog will follow your hand, the neck will bend, and the instinct to sit will automatically kick in.

For "come," we recommend clapping a hand against your chest.

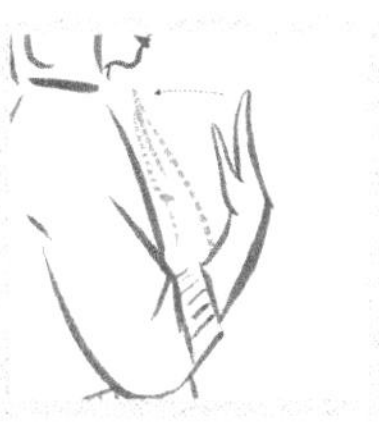

After two mornings of playing like this, Fred is making great progress, and Ovidiu can see the wheels turning. On several occasions, Fred even preempts Ovidiu by sitting and coming before he is encouraged to do so, which is the first sign that he is getting ready for the next stage of teaching. Later that afternoon when Ovidiu practices again with Fred, the connections and progress aren't as obvious, but Ovidiu doesn't dismay. He knows that a good night's sleep will refresh Fred, and they resume again the next morning.

 The Next Morning.

Have you ever worked at an academic or work-related problem for hours, given up in frustration, then awoken the next morning with the answers? Dogs often go through a similar experience with training. Don't get frustrated if you think your pup has finally grasped a concept only to lose it moments later. Play a little while, wrap up the training session, then be amazed the next morning when you practice again. Having had time to rest and refresh, when the sun comes up your pup will impress you with all that she has learned.

TEACHING STAGE 2:
USING A COMMAND

In a Nutshell —

Your dog now associates the actions of coming and sitting with the commands you have been using during play. You will gradually tone down encouragement and play when using the "come" and "sit" commands, and the commands start to be given in advance of the action (rather than while your dog is already performing the action).

The Process —

For a seasoned trainer, identifying when a dog is beginning to associate a command and gesture with an action is second nature, but the timing takes practice. In his third training session (though it will vary from dog to dog), Fred gives signs that he is linking the actions, language, and gestures for "sit" and "come." During their training games, Fred has been **consistently coming** when Ovidiu moves backwards, and Fred has been **preempting** Ovidiu by sitting at his feet before being encouraged to do so. Ovidiu notices that he gets very few misfires — Fred understands the game; his actions are dependable; and he is ready for more.

Ovidiu begins the second stage of teaching with "sit" (not "come") because the former is easier to learn and easier to enforce. Ovidiu is playing with Fred, moving backwards, and Fred is running towards him. As we mentioned, Fred has been preempting Ovidiu by sitting as soon as he reaches Ovidiu, so **this time Ovidiu preempts Fred**. Fred is about to reach Ovidiu, and just before he begins moving into the sit position, Ovidiu says "sit" and gives the hand gesture. Fred sits, and **Ovidiu gives immediate, much more enthusiastic praise, and a bigger reward — but only after the act — in this case sitting — is completed**.

The verbal praise for obeying the command is very excited, much more so than when Ovidiu was coaxing Fred into the sit position with treats and toys.

If you have chosen your moment well, like Ovidiu has with Fred, you will get the same result. Ovidiu set Fred up for success by paying close attention. Because Fred had been preempting Ovidiu's enticements to sit, he was likely to do so again, so Ovidiu used the command at just the right moment, before Fred began the action of sitting. Now, Fred begins to learn that the action follows the command. If your pup doesn't sit at the first attempt of using the command, go back to playing. You may have moved too fast. In addition, many dogs will sit the first time you try the command if they are ready, but the next time you try it they won't. This is normal. With practice, consistency will improve. After Fred sits and is rewarded for sitting, Ovidiu gives Fred a release command like, "okay go play," and they play for one or two minutes.

Throughout obedience training, you will be teaching your dog a release command in addition to "come" "sit" and "stay." The release command is your way of communicating to your dog that you no longer expect her to stay in the position you have asked her to take. If she is sitting or lying down, she is free to get up.

After this brief break, the "sit" command is practiced again, and the process is repeated. Gradually, Ovidiu transitions from using the command when Fred expects it, to using the "sit" command even when Fred does not expect it. All of the things that Ovidiu was doing to get Fred to sit — the games, the treats, the enthusiastic movements — will be dropped one by one until Fred is responding solely to the command for "sit." Training is incremental, and each step builds on what has already been learned. Over the course of the next 1-3 morning training sessions, Fred will learn to consistently and dependably sit in the quiet and comfortable environment of the park.

Once Fred is sitting consistently, Ovidiu introduces the concept of "stay" to Fred. This is how: with Fred sitting in front of him, Ovidiu shows Fred that he has a treat, puts it in his palm, and keeps his hand in front of Fred's nose (but not so close that Fred takes the treat). Ovidiu then says "stay" in a calm, elongated voice, and with his free hand introduces the gesture for "stay" which is a flat hand, palm facing out. Ovidiu then begins to move his body, walking a couple of steps from side to side, while keeping his hand in the same position in front of Fred. At this point, some dogs will instinctively follow the trainer instead of remaining seated. Fred makes a move to follow Ovidiu, so Ovidiu says "Fred, sit," and tries again. This time Ovidiu only takes one step in either direction and Fred remains sitting. He gets praise and the treat, then the release command.

In this way, incrementally, Ovidiu will work towards walking in a full circle around Fred while holding the treat steady in front of Fred's face and saying "stay." Every time Fred gets up, he is asked to "sit" again and then "stay" while Ovidiu moves. When Fred stays the whole time that Ovidiu walks around him, he is rewarded with the treat. The next step is for Ovidiu to walk over and around Fred by lifting his leg and stepping over Fred's back. If Fred startles or stands up, Ovidiu will take this step gradually by holding his leg up a little, then bit by bit, moving it over Fred's back until Fred stays sitting, focusing on the treat, while Ovidiu steps over and around.

Fred is learning to associate the "stay" command with remaining seated, even as Ovidiu moves. Once the association is made, Ovidiu can put the treat in his pocket when he walks around Fred instead of holding it in front of Fred's nose. If Fred gets up, Ovidiu immediately commands Fred to "sit" and he tries again. Through repetition and practice, the concept solidifies. It will take several months for "sit" *and* "stay" to be fully linked, meaning Ovidiu will only use the "sit" command instead of needing to ask Fred to sit and stay. Even once Fred has mastered "sit-stay," the "stay" command will be used intermittently to reinforce it.

Throughout the process of teaching Fred to sit and to stay, Ovidiu has been continuing to practice "come" in a casual way by using the command and gesture when Fred moves towards him in play. Now that Fred is ready, Ovidiu repeats the same process he used with "sit" to teach "come" with the expectation that Fred will respond with obedience. It's important to reinforce here, however, that moving from Teaching Stage 1 (associating the desired action with a word and gesture) to Teaching Stage 2 (using a command) is incremental and dependent on each dog's personality and progress. Ovidiu begins the transition by toning down his voice and movements a bit more each time Fred moves towards him. For example, at the beginning Ovidiu would run backwards quickly, playfully engaging Fred in play to entice him to follow. Now Ovidiu moves in a calmer way, and as Fred follows, the way Ovidiu says "come" and taps his chest a bit firmer and less playful. If Ovidiu was using a toy or treat to encourage Fred to come, at this stage he gradually stops doing so. As Fred learns to "come" with fewer enticements, the rewards are increased. The process continues until, when Ovidiu sees that Fred is ready, he stands in one place, firmly asks Fred to "come" with voice and gesture and expects that Fred will respond with obedience.

When Fred comes, he is rewarded with amped-up praise and a couple of minutes of play before trying again. For dogs more motivated by food, a bigger food reward would be given. Just as with the "sit" command, "come" will be practiced in the quiet corner of the park, with minimal distractions, until consistency is achieved. If your pup does not come, you probably moved too fast. Pick up the leash, move backwards, make your pup move towards you, then play and try again a few minutes later. During this period Ovidiu will also start using the "come" command when Fred is not expecting it — when he is relaxed and taking a break or playing. This is another important way to check Fred's progress.

At this stage, all teaching is positive. Ovidiu has done his due diligence and knows what rewards best incentivize Fred. But positive training and reinforcement only work if Fred perceives the rewards as accessible, if the goal is easily achievable. When teaching and practicing "sit-stay" and "come" with Fred, Ovidiu ***sets him up for success*** and makes sure he has plenty of opportunities to do what he is asked and get the rewards. Use of the commands is interspersed with play, and at the beginning Fred will not respond every single time. However, as Fred's reliability in responding improves, Ovidiu will gradually begin putting a little bit of distance between himself and Fred because it has become obvious that Fred understands the concept of being told to "sit-stay" and "come." This distance is, in fact, the first step of the Proofing phase in training.

 STRESS AND FATIGUE.

If your dog is showing signs of stress, fatigue, or distractedness it is time to either wrap up the training session or go back to some basic play. Your pup cannot learn when stressed or tired, nor do you want her to associate negative feelings with the training session. Always watch for these signs.

PROOFING PHASE:

In the proofing phase, Ovidiu is gradually going to introduce difficulty and distractions, using the following guidelines:

BABY STEPS:

Fred understands that in a specific environment like the quiet corner of the park he is expected to sit-stay and to come when Ovidiu asks. However, dogs are not very good at generalizing, and in this phase of training Ovidiu has to teach Fred that even in different environments and with different distractions, he is still expected to respond to the commands. In order to continue setting him up for success, difficulty is added incrementally, in baby steps.

ONE DISTRACTION AT A TIME:

Ovidiu will never introduce more than one new distraction or level of difficulty at a time. Once a distraction is mastered it can be paired with another distraction that has also already been mastered independently. For example, Ovidiu will proof "come" with Fred in a new place (first distraction) like the dog park at off-hours when he is unlikely to come across any other dogs. The secondary distraction (other dogs) is only added once Fred is comfortable and obedient in a relatively empty dog park.

ENFORCEMENTS:

It is also in the proofing phase that Ovidiu will introduce enforcements when they are needed. Fred is not going to respond to the command every time, especially as more and more distractions are introduced, and Ovidiu is going to use enforcement as a tool to show Fred that sitting and coming are still expected of him.

Ovidiu begins proofing "come" and "sit-stay" with Fred in the same quiet corner of the park they have been practicing. *Proofing should always begin in the same place that a dog has been learning new commands.* Fred is wearing a lightweight, 30-foot lead that can drag on the ground without getting caught or tangled.

 When training any dog, it is important to use a leash until the dog has really mastered new commands, particularly the "come" command. With a long lead a dog feels the weight of it and recognizes that Mom or Dad still has control, even though you are not holding the lead. It will be easy to grab the leash if needed to keep your dog safe. At the beginning you will use a 15- or 30-foot leash, and as your pup improves you will switch to a 6-foot leash. When her response to "come" is dependable, you will switch again to a tab leash that is just a few inches long.

Again, it is morning, and Fred is excited to begin his training session, which he knows always begins with fun activity. After some warm-up play that integrates the commands Fred knows, Ovidiu asks Fred to "sit" and "stay." He begins walking around Fred in spiraling circles, while reinforcing the "sit-stay" commands. Ovidiu moves slowly, gradually widening the circles and thus the distance between himself and Fred.

This is the first new level of difficulty added in the proofing phase: *distance.* Throughout this exercise, Ovidiu is watching Fred carefully for the point at which Fred stops obeying the "sit-stay" command. We call this the ***Point of Disobedience***, and identifying it is a critical step in training. Ovidiu is walking slowly behind Fred, now at about ten feet away, and Fred decides he doesn't want to sit anymore. The moment Fred begins to stand up, Ovidiu says "hey!" in his tough voice, picks up the leash, and gives it a quick snap. Fred stops and looks at Ovidiu, who then puts Fred in the sit position, in the same exact spot that he first asked Fred to sit, facing in the same direction, all while reinforcing the "sit-stay" command.

 The purpose of proofing is to work with your dog on dependent obedience given the distractions that are most relevant to your lifestyle. For example, a hunter who uses her dog to follow game will emphasize proofing commands at great distances. Her dog must be dependable even when she is not in sight. Most urban dog parents need dependent obedience in dog runs and city parks. Proofing will involve distractions like toys, other dogs, lots of noise, squirrels, and birds.

Fred's Point of Disobedience is when Ovidiu is behind him and about ten feet away, so Ovidiu will work at this point until Fred consistently stays when asked. Then Ovidiu will gradually progress to eleven feet, fifteen feet, twenty feet and so on, incrementally increasing difficulty only when Fred has mastered the command at the previous level. Ovidiu uses the same process for proofing the "come" command, and this practice is integrated with "sit-stay."

 When proofing or practicing a command, *you get two tries with the verbal command in case your pup was distracted, but only two.* More than that and you risk watering down the command and teaching your puppy that when you say "come" she doesn't really have to listen. For example, you ask Luna to come, but she doesn't seem to have heard you. You will say her name and the command one more time, a little louder and a little firmer. If she doesn't respond, yet you are sure she heard you, you will enforce the command.

Once Ovidiu is working with Fred at a distance that exceeds the length of the lead, enforcing a command can become more difficult, but the principles remain the same. If Fred's lead is out of reach and he refuses to come or gets up from the sit position before he is released, Ovidiu will use his voice first, as always, and if that doesn't get Fred's attention he will have to move towards Fred and get ahold of the lead. No matter how long this takes, Ovidiu will continue the enforcement uninterrupted. Remember that continuity means that even if Fred moves away, *Ovidiu will continue to use his voice to express his displeasure until he can catch Fred's lead and command Fred's attention.*

In the same *incremental* way that Ovidiu introduces distance to Fred in proofing "come" and "sit-stay" (but not at the same time), he introduces a ball as the second distraction. Ovidiu asks Fred to "sit-stay" then he takes a ball from his pocket and shows it to Fred. He slowly increases the distraction by bouncing the ball, moving it in front of Fred then away, and finally throwing the ball. Throughout, he reinforces the "sit-stay" command and watches for Fred's Point of Disobedience. It doesn't take long. At the start, the distraction of the ball proves too tempting for Fred when Ovidiu bounces it. Fred jumps up to try to catch the ball, and Ovidiu immediately gets his attention with "hey" and a snap of the leash. He places Fred in the sit position then practices again, working with Fred at staying even when the ball is bouncing, gradually increasing the difficulty as Fred becomes more obedient. By now, this process should sound familiar. By the end of the training session, Fred stays seated, even when Ovidiu throws the ball over his head.

Over the next few days, Ovidiu will proof the "come" and "sit-stay" commands with Fred in new places and with new distractions. Fred is an urban pup who also goes for hikes, so Ovidiu teaches Fred — in baby steps — that he must have a dependent response to these commands both from a distance and when playing in crowded parks that are full of distractions like other dogs, food, toys, kids, birds, cars, and squirrels.

 Remember, as you expand the scope of difficulty you should only add or change one thing at a time, and only after your dog has mastered the command in a new setting. For example, the first time you practice "sit-stay" from a distance of 20 feet, don't also introduce the distraction of a ball.

As Fred gets better and better at generalizing the commands he has learned, Ovidiu will begin weaning him off of rewards — they will become ***intermittent***. This means that Fred will not get a reward every time he obeys a command, and there will be no predictable pattern. As Fred gets older and more experienced, Ovidiu may go a few hours without rewarding Fred with a treat. Fred knows that once in a while he will get a piece of hot dog, but because the timing is spontaneous, he doesn't expect a treat every time. Praise as a reward will also become intermittent, but it will be used more than treats.

 Intermittent Rewards. At the point when you feel your dog has mastered the concept of the command and is usually responsive in different environments, you are going to start an alternate schedule of intermittent praise and treats. This means that you will no longer be giving your dog a reward every time she sits, and the schedule for rewards is always variable. Intermittent rewards are given somewhere between never and always, with the frequency decided by you. You will be guided by your dog's dependability and how often you practice commands.

MAINTENANCE PHASE:

Practice! Incorporate all obedience training that has been taught and proofed into everyday activities. We often hear from parents that they do not have time for daily practice, but even a few minutes is valuable and essential.

REPEATING THE PROCESS WITH OTHER COMMANDS:

Once you understand the process and the principles that underlie each stage of obedience training, you will be able to teach your dog whatever commands you think are important. The steps are the same for all commands: teaching (through play, introduce the action you will later command; associate a word, gesture, and reward with the desired action; then, use the word and gesture as a command); proofing (gradually introduce distractions to increase responsiveness and dependability to the command); and maintenance.

However, you will need to tailor the way you play, the gestures you use, the way you proof, and the way you practice each specific command to the personality of your dog.

OBEDIENCE TRAINING: WALK ON A LEASH

A dog who knows how to properly walk on a leash will trot along at a pace that roughly matches yours; she will be curious about her surroundings but more attentive to and engaged with you; she'll stop when you stop, turn when you turn, and go when you say "let's go"; she won't put on the brakes or pull ahead.

Properly walking on a leash is not the same as "heeling" (a command that requires your dog to stay at your side whether in motion or still, leashed or not leashed).

Rather, properly walking on a leash describes a dog who enjoys her walks and abides by the walking rules that you have established.

The approach to training any dog to be a delightful, leashed companion is two-pronged and straightforward. You will

1) encourage your dog to move with you and

2) discourage your dog from pulling.

Of course, success depends on getting the details right, so we'll spend this section teaching you how to get your dog to move in the right way and how to stop her from moving in the wrong way.

THE FOUNDATIONS:

The process begins (no surprises here) with the same basic principles that precede all obedience training: play, a positive relationship, and clear communication. From the moment you bring your dog home, you will be encouraging her to follow you and be attuned to you.

If you are engaged with her, she will be engaged with you. You will practice leashed walks, and you will make them fun and reward her engagement with play, praise, and treats on your outings. Use positive encouragement and start associating her movement with the "let's go" command.

"LET'S GO" AND "EASY":

"Let's go" is an important command that doesn't exactly mean "come." It means "move in the same direction as me, walk with me, and pay attention to where and how I am moving." You will use "let's go" before your pup knows how to respond to a proper "come" command. It is more casual. Your pup will respond to "let's go" because you are fun and interesting. Even after your dog has learned the "come" command, you will continue to use "let's go" in a number of situations. For example, when you want her to walk next to you on the leash or follow you on an off-leash adventure while hiking. In general, "come" will be used when you are stationary and you want your dog to come to the spot where you are standing, then "sit-stay." "Let's go" will be used when you are moving and you want your pup to join you in motion.

"Easy" is your way of communicating to your pup that you need her to take it down a notch. You will use "easy" if she starts to pull or move too fast.

THE WALK:

When your pup enjoys playing with you and loves going for walks, she will be excited when she sees the leash. Once you have it attached, you'll say "let's go" and that should be enough to get her moving. If she puts on the brakes, you haven't done your job, and you'll need to ramp up your positive encouragement. Sometimes puppies and adult dogs in a new environment can be stubbornly stationary on the leash, but patience, practice, and positive incentives will eventually win any dog over. Once your pup starts moving, your next job will be to show her limits.

PULLING IS CORRECTED:

When a dog is about six months old, we treat pulling as any other bad habit like jumping or chewing. The moment she pulls on the leash you will use a firm "hey" or "easy" with a quick snap of the leash to communicate your displeasure and to command her attention. She will learn that instead of pulling ahead on the leash, she is expected to move in synchronization with you, paying attention to your speed and direction. She has some freedom to move around in front of you or behind you, stopping to sniff and look about if you slow down, but she knows she cannot pull the leash. If a leash snap is not enough (and it often isn't), you will change course and walk briskly in a different direction. Whatever your pup is pulling toward, you'll make sure she doesn't get there. She will learn that pulling never achieves its desired purpose, and if you are consistent, she will slow down as soon as you say "easy."

Following these tips and teaching your pup how to properly walk on a leash is not just for your comfort but for hers as well. There will be no need for harnesses that impede her mobility or battles of tug-the-leash on the street. You will be able to keep her safe, and you will both enjoy your jaunty sidewalk strolls.

CHAPTER 11

BEHAVIORAL PROBLEMS

In this book, we have focused on the right ways to raise a happy and balanced pup in an urban environment. By implementing a healthy, holistic lifestyle for your dog and by following our puppy and obedience training guidelines, you should be able to preempt any serious behavioral problems. Aggression and ingrained bad habits are the two categories that most behavioral problems fall within, and a guide to managing them is well outside the purview of this book; however, if unwanted behaviors do arise, we think it is important that parents are able to identify their source.

UNDERSTANDING WHY A DOG IS BEHAVING the way she is, is the first step in being able to properly manage the behavior. A dog who chews up the sofa because she has separation anxiety, for example, requires an entirely different remedy than a sofa-chewing dog with an overabundance of energy who may just need more exercise and stimulation. Our hope is that by using the information here to identify and intervene early, you will be able to nip any problems in the bud and raise a balanced pup.

BAD HABITS

Bad habits are unwanted behaviors like jumping on people, chewing, and too much barking. We call them "habits" because these behaviors are learned — the dog has been allowed to repeat the behavior over and over again without a parent intervening, and a habit has formed. When we refer to bad habits, we are not talking about behaviors that stem from fear or stress.

STEP 1: INTERVENE BEFORE THE BEHAVIOR BECOMES AN INGRAINED HABIT —

Often, bad habits develop during puppyhood because things like jumping can look really cute in mini-version, and by the time Mom or Dad realizes that 75 pounds of dog can knock a person down, the behavior has become ingrained. But bad habits can be picked up at any point in a dog's life, and regardless of how old the dog is, the more immediate your intervention the better odds you have of preventing the behavior from becoming an ingrained habit. If ignored, the problem will require much more time and effort to change.

Example:
Joe and Pip are lab-mix puppies and are brother and sister. Both have a penchant for chewing socks, but they are adopted by different families who deal with the bad habit in different ways. Joe's family immediately removes the socks and redirects Joe's attention to toys he is allowed to chew on. Redirection was enough for Joe (as it often is at this young age), and on the

one or two occasions he sniffed out a sock, a short verbal "hey" was enough to deter him from putting his mouth on it. By the time Joe grew out of his teething phase, socks were a thing of the past. Pip's family didn't deal with the sock chewing right away because they thought it was pretty cute and her little mouth didn't really do any damage. But as Pip grew, she began to destroy socks and eventually moved on to other soft furnishings in the house. The habit became learned, ingrained.

STEP 2: EXTINGUISH THE INGRAINED HABIT USING NEGATIVE STIMULI —

Whether it is a new behavior or an old habit, the two-fold principle for extinguishing the behavior is the same. First, when you are home and can observe your dog, present her with the opportunity to make a choice between good and bad behavior. You want her to have the chance to do the right thing and get rewarded. But, if she makes the wrong choice, be vigilant and consistent in correcting bad behavior as soon as it starts to happen. Second, when you cannot keep a careful eye on your pup, remove the opportunity to misbehave. Eventually your little one will understand that the behavior is unacceptable in any context and you will be able to trust her to roam the house freely in your absence. However, you do have to make it clear that the behavior is unacceptable.

Example:
Lola likes to help herself to food from the kitchen. She is an agile and leggy boxer who not only clears the counters but also likes to poke around the cabinets. This is one of the toughest

bad habits to break because the reward for misbehaving — a stomach full of yummies — is huge, and the bigger the reward for misbehavior the harder it is to implement an effective negative consequence. Lola's personality is also a factor; a sensitive dog may learn quickly that an approach to the counter will be met with a stern "hey" from Mom, and cease the behavior, but not Lola. Lola's parents have to offer a tap on the nose or quick yank of the collar together with a tough vocal command like, "No, Lola, bad dog!" in order to deter her.

Mom and Dad begin by leaving some really appetizing goodies on the counter, something with a strong aroma like bacon, and then wait for Lola to make her move. It is important that Lola never actually gets her paws on the bacon during training because that will be a pretty big incentive to continue the habit. It will be alluringly placed on the counter, but unbeknownst to Lola, quite out of reach. If Lola is reluctant to jump on the counter in plain sight, Mom and Dad will leave the kitchen area but keep a close eye on their pup. For example, they will pretend to leave the room or home but actually be watching from around the corner. As soon as she jumps up, she is immediately corrected. Mom swiftly enters the room using her corrective word like "hey," pulls Lola off the counter, and taps her nose with displeased posture. If Lola is still reaching for the goodies during the correction, the message is not being clearly communicated and received. Lola's response to a proper correction that she understands will be to stop the unwanted behavior and give you her undivided attention. The process is repeated until Lola understands that every time she jumps on the counter, instead of a stomach full of yummies, she gets mad Mom or Dad. The bacon will gradually be moved closer and closer to Lola until, even when it is right on the edge of the table, she doesn't try to take it. When she can't be supervised, access to the kitchen is limited during this training process because consistency is key. Lola has to be met with negative consequences every single time she attempts the misbehavior. The more ingrained the behavior, the longer it will take to stop.

Eventually, Lola will associate countertop cruising with a negative stimulus instead of a reward, and she can be trusted to keep her paws to herself even when Mom and Dad are not home.

AGGRESSION

WHAT IS AGGRESSION?

Aggression is when a dog ***intentionally harms, attempts to harm, or threatens to harm*** another dog or person.

Bear with us while we parse the language. Intentionally harms means that the dog has to actually do the harm on purpose. A play bite that accidentally causes injury is not aggression. However, even something as small as a growl or posture can be an act of aggression if the dog is warning or threatening another dog with harm. In fact, most acts of aggression that we see are threats. Aggression can be a growl, a lunge, a bite, or a full-on attack. Dogs exhibit these behaviors for a number of reasons, and we'll cover the main ones here.

1. FEAR AND STRESSOR-BASED AGGRESSION

This is the most common kind of aggression we see, and in fact, it is normal for any dog to respond to a certain level of stress with aggression.

> Misconception:
> "My dog would never bite."
>
> Wrong. Even the calmest, most well-behaved pup will have a point at which she snaps in a stressful situation, whether it is because the veterinarian is giving her a painful injection, a pack of dogs has cornered her in the dog run, or she is defending herself when another dog attacks.

Fear and stressor-based aggression become problematic when a dog reacts to normal, everyday stimuli with aggression or when her reactions are unpredictable. The urban environment is a breeding ground for fear-based aggression for two reasons: dogs are more likely to be confronted with stressors, and they are more likely to have pent-up energy.

2. LEARNED HABIT AGGRESSION

Aggression can be a learned habit just like any other bad habit, but the consequences are much more serious. The typical cases of aggression as a learned habit are dogs who like to lunge at other dogs on a leashed walk, or dogs who chase and bite other dogs in places like the dog park when other stress-related factors are not present. Habits form when a dog gets some sort of initial reward or pleasure from a specific action: behaving in a dominant manner, aggressively lunging on the leash, or biting dogs in the dog run can, to the dismay of most parents, be really exhilarating for some dogs. Sometimes, an initial aggressive reaction that was provoked by fear becomes a learned habit.

We often see learned aggression in small dogs because when the initial behavior occurred, it did not seem dangerous enough for Mom or Dad to take seriously. The food-possessive Yorkie or the Lhasa Apso who won't let anyone else on the bed are typical examples of pups who have learned to bite. These pups used aggression and got the result they wanted — i.e., got to stay on the bed or keep the food. Through consistent reinforcement, the pups learned that they had a specific kind of power, and the aggressive behavior became ingrained. These dogs are often described as "feisty" by their parents, but in truth, their behaviors are aggressive.

Misconception:

"My dog isn't aggressive; she's just being protective."

The scenario: Fresh Direct delivers the week's groceries, and Lulu lunges at the delivery man when he tries to enter the house. It's okay, she's just being protective? No. She may be acting from an impulse to protect, but the action is nonetheless aggressive.

 Aggression is aggression, whether or not the impetus is possessive, protective, or fear based. There are certain behaviors that may be mistaken for aggression that are, in fact, benign, but interpreting oneself or one's family as the object of protection cannot be used to redefine aggressive behavior as non-aggressive. Importantly, if not corrected in time, the aggression will become more dangerous and more frequent. A snarl at guests entering the house can become a snap or a bite, and the dog will eventually resort to these aggressive behaviors in a broader range of situations such as on the street or in the park.

3. TRAINED AGGRESSION

Dogs are trained to be aggressive for a number of purposes, the most common being working dogs trained for protection (home guarding, police work), and dogs trained to fight one another for illegal sport. Training your dog to be aggressive is absolutely not something you should consider. Sport fighting is inhumane in any context, and if you are one of a select group of individuals qualified to train working dogs for protection you are probably not reading this book.

WHAT ISN'T AGGRESSION?

Aggression is not defined by the results of a certain behavior, but by the intention behind the behavior. Therefore, if a dog or person is injured or frightened by another dog's behavior, but that behavior was accidental or misinterpreted, it is not aggression. Importantly, loud play is not aggression. It can be very difficult for parents to decipher aggression from excitement and play, particularly when dogs are interacting in high-energy environments. Even for the experienced eye, the line from fun to fight can be crossed before anyone has the chance to put a pause on the games. However, most of the time when dogs are chasing each other, barking, wrestling, and jumping, they are safely playing.

When a dog is barking at another dog to try to engage her in play, this is not aggression (it sounds obvious, but we cannot count how many times we have seen parents accuse another dog of being aggressive at the dog run when, in fact, the pup just wanted someone to play with). Taking another dog's toy or playing tug o' war is not aggression. When puppies chew on your fingers this is not aggression.

Learning what is and what is not healthy play takes practice and experience. For more information on decoding play, skip ahead to the City Living section.

HOW IS AGGRESSION FIXED?

1. PREVENTION

Addressing aggression is one of the biggest challenges for parents because it takes commitment and expertise to extinguish it. Therefore, the best thing to do is stop it at the outset — take any sign of aggression seriously and don't let it become an ingrained behavior. You will deal with early stages of aggression in the same way you would any other bad habit, by meeting the unwanted behavior with a negative consequence. Lunging on the leash is met with a forceful "hey" and a quick snap of the leash; nipping triggers the same "hey" communication of displeasure, tough body language, and a tap on the nose while holding your pup's collar; if a large dog growls at a person passing by, the consequence may be lifting her up by the collar so that she is immobilized and only her back feet are on the ground while you communicate that her behavior is unacceptable.

In addition to triggering a negative consequence, it's critical that there is no reward associated with her aggressive behaviors. If your pup nips because she wants something, like a spot on the bed or the food on the table, make sure you take that thing away at the same time that you impose a negative consequence.

If you are attuned to your dog, take the first signs of aggression seriously, and consistently impose a meaningful, negative consequence for unacceptable behavior, you will be able to raise a balanced and well-behaved pup. For some dogs, however, the problem has already become ingrained, and in this situation we recommend consulting an expert.

2. CONSULT AN EXPERT

If the problem is serious, most parents should turn to a professional trainer for advice and help. Even for an experienced dog trainer, however, managing aggression can be a difficult undertaking. In the case of fear and stressor-based aggression, most trainers will use a version of exposure therapy to try and get your pup used to and comfortable with whatever stimulates her aggression.

If you decide to reach out to a trainer, make sure you find someone who is comfortable with and experienced addressing aggressive behaviors. While it is always important to do your research when entrusting the care or training of your dog to someone else, in the case of aggression your trainer's experience is of the utmost importance.

The most practical solution for most parents of dogs with ingrained aggressive behaviors is to adapt home, lifestyle, environment, or all three in order to keep everyone safe. The principle is pretty straightforward — if you can't take the fight out of the dog, take the dog out of the fight! If she is nippy with kids, keep her away from kids; if she snaps while eating, give her a private space in which to eat; if she bites other dogs, don't take her to the dog run.

One of the easiest ways to adapt is to use a muzzle when appropriate. Soft, nylon muzzles are often sufficient and allow your dog to breathe comfortably and drink water. They can't be left on all the time but are really effective for the times when your pup is faced with the thing that stimulates her aggression like kids or other dogs. Don't let the stigma of the muzzle (and the looks of judgment from other people) stop you from doing what is best for your dog.

PART IV

CITY LIVING

CHAPTER 12

DOG PARK ETIQUETTE

After living in New York for more than twenty years, we've seen a lot of what this city has to offer: the good and the bad, the beautiful and the ugly, the ordered and the chaotic. And yet, in this vast and diverse urban habitat, the most unexpected, blood-pressure-raising, irrational interactions, have occurred in the dog park.

THE DOG PARK IS A MICROCOSM of city life. People and their pets of all different shapes and sizes, temperaments and backgrounds are trying to get along and share resources in a small space. If done right, the result is beautiful: new friends are made, social lives flourish, news is shared, and everyone is stimulated. But when toes are stepped on here (literally and figuratively) things can sour quickly. The dogs are pretty good at figuring out their differences and not taking stuff personally, but their human counterparts often have a bit of evolving to do on that front. The most belligerent interactions — and we are not kidding here, we've seen them end with calls to the police — usually occur when someone feels their pup has been insulted. Think you've seen it all? Go to the dog run and tell someone that their dog is a jerk.

We are not trying to scare you away from the dog runs, we love them! Seriously, this advice is coming from a couple whose dog park meeting led to marriage and kids. We just want you to be prepared. If you know the rules, the etiquette, and understand both canine and human dog park behavior, you and your doggy will be much more likely to have a fun experience. We've put together a list below of the important dog park rules so you will be well armed to make the most of your trips to the urban dog run.

OPEN AND CLOSE THE GATES, ONE AT A TIME

Most dog runs have two gates on either side of a small vestibule and some even have separate entrance and exit areas. Follow the rules because they are there for a reason! Unless you want to experience the wrath of other park patrons, the number one rule is to open and close one gate at a time so no little trouble-making fur-balls escape. And trust us, they will escape!

IF YOU BRING A TOY, IT'S COMMUNAL PROPERTY

"Um, could you please tell your dog to stop chasing my dog's frisbee?" We have heard a version of this implicit reproach and ridiculous question more times than you'd like to believe. To state the obvious, you could tell your dog to stop chasing Luna's frisbee, but she probably isn't going to listen. Nor should she. Once it is released into the dog run, whatever toy is bouncing around or flying through the air is fair game.

It is not okay to place an additional burden on other patrons of the dog run by asking them to make sure their dog doesn't snatch Fido's special toy, and if that does happen, to require them to take the toy from their dog's mouth and bring it back to you over and over again. To the other pups in the dog run, it's not "Luna's ball" or "Kona's ball," it's just a fun toy.

It is okay to bring a toy to the dog run, allow it to be shared, and then politely retrieve it to take home with you before leaving. But, if it's a special toy that your pup is likely to be possessive over, don't bring it. If it's expensive and you don't want it to get chewed on or peed on, don't bring it.

DON'T BRING A CHILD

Small children have no place in the dog run. If you bring a child, she will get jumped on. Even if that's "fine" by you because your little one is a toughie, it is not fair to the other dogs and parents in the park. Kids are unpredictable and dogs are wary of this unpredictability; kids get excited and dogs react to this excitement. Most parents know this and will be immediately on guard or even feel they have to leave the dog run to avoid an uncomfortable situation. Children + dog run = disaster and we've seen it more times than we can count. It usually ends up with a child crying, a dog being punished, and ashamed dog parents dragging their over-excited pups out of the park.

PEOPLE, DON'T RUN UNLESS YOU WANT TO GET CHASED

Better yet, don't run in the dog park. You are not a dog. The dogs think it's weird because it is, and if they aren't weirded out by it, they are probably going to chase you. "I just want my little cutie to run some laps and burn some energy like we do at home! Why are all these giants barking at my heels?" Because that's what dogs do; it's their instinct. You run, they will chase. It will be chaotic. Save this game for off-leash hours in the regular park, when you and your pup have more space.

DON'T BE INTERFERING AND UNIFORMED

> Misconception:
> A Panting Dog Is Overheating and Needs Water

It's true that dogs pant when they are hot, and it's also true that your dog should have access to plenty of water. But panting, in and of itself, is a way for dogs to cool their body temperature; it is how they "sweat." Panting is not a state of discomfort caused by thirst, and tongue-hanging-out-of-mouth is not your dog's way of asking for a drink of water. Rather, that tongue needs to be exposed to *air*. By opening the mouth, breathing heavily, and letting her tongue hang long, your dog is using the air to cool her body temperature.

The tongue provides more surface area for moisture to evaporate and more blood vessels to be cooled, a process which helps to circulate cooler blood throughout the head and body, controlling her body temperature. If she is thirsty and water is available, she will drink; there is no need to shove water in her face.

> Misconception:
> Barking Is Aggressive

The scenario: Last week they played like besties, this week Bella won't stop barking at Buddy. Frenemies? No, likely just friends. Barks, like wags, have different meanings in different situations. One of the most frequently misinterpreted barks is the play bark. Parents must learn to become familiar with their dog's particular noises; barks for play sound different than barks for warning, begging, and aggression. Read the sounds together with body language like posturing, raised hair, and ear positioning, and you will quickly learn to understand the whole story.

Our Emma has a "huff" for needing to go out; a deeper "huff" for coming in; a whiny bark for "feed me"; a loud, enthusiastic bark for play; a growl followed by a sharp and nasty snap-bark for aggression; a long howl for "someone's at the door"; a short, soprano yip for "don't tease me, mom"; and a drama-queen-diva yelp for "you stepped on my foot!" It sounds complicated, but it's not. It's a vocabulary of eight words.

> Misconception:
> A Shaking Dog Needs a Coat

Oh, if we could count how many times a passerby has

scowled, tskked at us, threatened to call the police because our poor shaking Ollie was not wearing a coat in 50-degree weather . . . It's hard to bite one's tongue in this situation, but we usually do because really, why should we have to take time away from our pups' walk to explain to a stranger that our beloved little Ollie shakes when he is cold, but he also shakes when he is excited and happy? That he shakes when it's 70 degrees and sunny? That our little dude would rather run in the snow on a cold day without a coat because he finds clothing silly and constricting? Dogs shake for lots of reasons: sometimes they are old, sometimes they are excited, and yes, sometimes they are cold. But please remember that unless it's a Chinese crested dog, pups come with their own fur coats and they don't usually want or need anything else.

> Misconception:
> A Wagging Tail Is a Happy Dog

The Scenario: Two dogs walk toward each other on the street, meet, and a fight breaks out. The parents exclaim in surprise, "But they were wagging their tails!"

If there exists a human counterpart for a tail wag, we might say it is when the corners of our mouth turn up into a smile. Sometimes I smile because I'm happy or excited and when I want to make others feel welcome; I also have smiles to ridicule, condescend, deride, or reproach; to hide my nerves, and to suggest that I'm about to lash out in anger. It sounds like a language filled with indecipherable subterfuge, but you, as a fellow human, are remarkably adept at reading the nuances of my facial expressions.

Like the human smile, messages sent from a dog's tail require complex code cracking best left to the canine eye. Most of us will have to settle for a more limited translation: wag does not always equal happy. Dogs wag their tails to show happiness, excitement, confidence, anger, and annoyance. A tail raised high usually marks alertness or caution, lower is more relaxed, but all the way between the legs can mean submission or anxiety. You don't have to be an expert as long as you know that a wag can mean something other than "life is a blissful adventure" because it will help you to prepare for potential bad behavior. If your dog has a history of biting puppies and she wags her tail when approached by one on the street, it probably doesn't mean that she suddenly overcame her grouchy disposition. Likewise, if your pup likes to meet new friends on her walks, don't assume that every furry beast with a wag means a new BFF. Be cautious.

EXPECT TO GET DIRTY (EVEN TO GET PEED ON)

We have very good friends who, after a life of living with dogs in rural Vermont, recently bought an apartment in the city and decided to visit an urban dog run for the very first time. They called us up to tell us about the adventure and in exasperation explained how one of them was PEED on, and could we believe it, and they would certainly not be taking Pepper back any time soon. Knowing us and our line of work they asked what the parent should have done in that situation — paid for dry cleaning? They were disappointed by our answer.

No, the parent should not pay for dry cleaning. In fact, by wearing fancy stuff you are placing yet another unfair burden on fellow users of the dog run. The dogs are there to have fun, run around freely, play, and get dirty.

While this doesn't mean that you also have to roll in the mud, you will probably suffer some collateral damage, and yes, you might even get peed on. The dog run is so filled with smells that to a lot of the pups roaming around reading the news, the leg on your body might just as well be the leg of the bench. Likewise, that expensive fur coat you draped across the fence might as well be the best dog toy ever invented, so don't be surprised if someone takes it for a spin around the park.

We are not suggesting anarchy in the dog run. Parents should be vigilant and try to minimize behaviors like peeing on people and stealing coats, but sometimes this stuff happens, and it's normal. Take prophylactic measures and just wear your yuckies to the dog run.

DON'T BRING FOOD (DOG OR HUMAN)

This is another one of those rules of etiquette that falls into the "don't create an extra burden for other patrons" category. The dog park is a place for play, activity, and exercise. As soon as you introduce food into the equation, the magic of the social atmosphere is interrupted. Snacks for the two-legged visitors are usually the worst offenders.

Bring a burger to the dog run and it will probably get snatched. If it doesn't get snatched you will be faced with a mob of drooling dogs who, once actively playing are now reacting to the stimulus of grilled meat smell that, no matter how hard their parents try to distract them with calls and balls, will overwhelm the brain.

Forgetting about the dog treats in your pocket is an excusable (and common) offense, but don't start doling them out. If you do, you'll have to start sharing and not only will you interrupt the social atmosphere, you might also anger some patrons whose dogs are vegan or sensitive to gluten or allergic to peanuts.

PICK UP POOP

The dog park is a communal space that everyone has an interest in keeping clean, so be on top of it. Try to always clean up after your pup, and if you are about to leave and realize you didn't see Fido poop, grab a bag and pick up someone else's. Pick up poop every time you go to the dog run, even if you aren't sure that it belongs to your pup, even if you are sure it *doesn't* belong to your pup. Why? Because you will be, more often than you will ever realize, negligent when it comes to catching your dog in the act.

Many dog runs also have local cleanup days where the community is encouraged to participate in an afternoon of doing the icky tasks that don't normally get done. If you use the dog run, put on some gloves and muck boots and take part. These community cleanups are absolutely essential for maintenance and hygiene. Plus, they are a great way to cement friendships with your fellow park-goers.

DON'T BURN BRIDGES

It's an easy mistake to make. As mentioned in the beginning of this section, the dog run is a place where emotions can run high: we've seen expletives hurled, physical intimidation, even police called over a loud game of chase. But if you ever get involved in a verbal tit-for-tat with a fellow dog run patron, just remember that he or she is probably not going to stop coming to the dog run.

People often bring their pup to a local dog run at the same time every day, and tomorrow you may find yourself sitting across the park from the person you called "crazy Tinker Bell" the day before (even though she did come to the dog run in a blue tutu and quite probably drunk).

PAY ATTENTION

The best way to avoid any dog park pitfalls and to help cultivate that social atmosphere we keep mentioning is simply to pay attention. If you sit down with your screen and expect your pup to take care of herself, you are in for disappointment and maybe even trouble.

Be vigilant, be engaged, be informed, and everyone will have fun!

CHAPTER 13

NOTES ON URBAN WALKS

The dog run is not the only place where you will need to be aware of hazards and how-to's specific to city life. The plain vanilla leashed walk comes with its own set of considerations:

TALL BUILDINGS —

CITY FOOTPRINTS TEND to be small, which means we move up and down for basic things like getting to the subway, the supermarket, or the rooftop dog park. Tall buildings are a fact of life in the urban environment, and they come with a few tricky things for pups to navigate: elevators, escalators, lots of stairs, and lots of construction. However, getting your dog used to this stuff is really just another facet of socialization, and by now you should be familiar with the approach. Expose your puppy to all the modes of going up and down, and if she shows signs of anxiety, take the process in baby steps while maintaining your calm and positive demeanor. Escalators and elevators can feel really weird to a dog, but she will get used to them like anything else. Remember not to reward anxiety with affection. Finally, a special note on elevators: never let your pup charge the elevator doors to get on or off. We have seen dog fights break out when a pup waiting by the elevator is met with an unfamiliar face as soon as the doors open or vice versa. Surprised dogs sometimes behave aggressively, even if they are normally balanced.

READING OTHER PEOPLE —

Our Emma does not like meeting puppies when she is on a leashed walk. We take appropriate measures by keeping her in a heel position and stepping off of the sidewalk when passing other energetic dogs, and while that should be enough, it is often not. Almost daily someone approaches saying, "Don't worry, my dog is friendly!" and bounds towards us as we move further and further away, placing our bodies between the oncoming ball of energy and our rather grouchy old lady. Please don't be so inconsiderate.

In addition to keeping control of your own dog, you have the responsibility of reading the people around you, particularly other people with pets. Do not allow your dog to approach another dog or person without being invited to do so. It does not matter if your pup is perfectly behaved and friendly; you are dealing with another being who could be scared, mean, sick, frail, aggressive, anxious, or injured. The invitation to interact does not have to be explicit, but it does have to be clear. Anyone in a dog run has issued an implicit invitation to interact, and the same goes for dog parents who let their pups run off leash during specifically designated park hours. However, when leashed dogs cross paths, parents should always communicate. "Can my dog say hi?" and "Is your dog friendly?" are two ways to ask permission. If you are approaching someone and they shorten their dog's leash, shield themselves or their dog with their body, or move to the edge of the sidewalk, they are communicating that they do not want to interact. It doesn't matter how friendly your dog is, it is your job to restrain her and avoid contact.

SHOPPING —

Many, many urban shops will allow you to bring your pup inside, and this is one more way that city living can really foster socialization and build community – especially in bookstores! We've made great friends strolling through The Strand and perusing the shelves at our neighborhood Greenlight Bookstore in Brooklyn. We encourage urban dog parents to do the same, keeping a few rules of etiquette in mind. While your pup is welcome, muddy paws, loud barks, and marking are not. Be mindful so that shops continue to welcome dogs and parents can enjoy the company of their pups on urban errands.

CITY HAZARDS —

Rat poison, feces, garbage, and broken glass are real hazards that are found on the streets and in the parks of most urban areas. Water in puddles, ponds, and lakes, is often polluted. Be mindful and attentive, but please don't let the fear mongers scare you into keeping your dog on a short leash, literally and metaphorically. Weigh the risks and rewards of certain activities and be mindful.

TETHERING —

Tethering, or tying your dog to something with the leash, should only be done under supervision. For example, you need two hands to pick up something off of the street, so you tie your dog to a post a few feet away. It is often tempting for city dwellers to tether their pups while they pop into the deli to get some milk or run upstairs to the apartment for something forgotten, but we caution against this. It doesn't matter how well behaved your own dog is, you cannot predict the behavior of other dogs and people. You are placing your pup in a very vulnerable position by immobilizing her. She is unable to defend herself or seek safety if an aggressive dog or nasty person passes by. If for some reason you find it necessary to tether your dog while she is unsupervised, please do not do so with a slip/choke collar. The risks are self-evident.

CHAPTER 14

DECODING PLAY

Learning to decipher what is play and what is not is something anyone can do, but having an introduction to dog behaviors can help, and practice is essential. Even pups themselves learn how to play through practice, ideally in that critical period for socialization from 3-16 weeks.

BEING PRACTICED IN DECODING basic doggy body language serves two purposes: first, parents need to be able to spot the early signs of discomfort or stress when their dog is engaged in a social interaction. The typical scenario occurs in a dog run when one pup is engaged in a game of chase with one or more other dogs. The parents' attention drifts and all of a sudden, Lola is cornered by the fence. Mikey is barking at her, anxious to continue the chase, but he isn't receiving Lola's signals. Her back is arched and she begins to bare her teeth because she feels trapped and intimidated. At this moment, a parent could intervene, throw the ball for a few minutes, and completely diffuse the situation by redirecting everyone's energy before a fight breaks out. The fights are obvious, but the initial warning signs are less so, and knowing when to intervene early will prevent a dangerous situation. It often happens quickly, but there are always signs.

Second, parents should know when not to intervene. Every day in the NYC dog runs we frequent, best buddies are pulled apart by their nervous parents for playing in a way that looks a little too wild or uncivilized. The pups are confused or disappointed because they are merely playing like dogs; they are not supposed to be civilized. Healthy play can sometimes look like fighting to the untrained eye, and we think this is one of the reasons we encounter so many dogs who have not been properly socialized. Parents are afraid of play — both because they don't want any four-legged park visitors getting hurt and because they don't want to offend the two-legged visitors. Fears of stepping on toes in a densely populated environment sometimes dominate everyday social interactions. But allowing pups to play, even if it is loud and chaotic, is integral to the emotional wellbeing and social education of your dog.

The first thing to look for when your dog is interacting with others, whether or not play is involved, are pro-social behaviors. These are little signals your dog is giving to another dog or dogs that mean something like, "I come in peace." You will see silly, puppy-like movements (they often look sloppy), licking, ears back, paws being raised, and whining.

Before play begins, you might see familiar invitations like a face that looks like a grin and the "play bow." All of these cues can be the first obvious signs that play is welcome and is about to begin, especially if both pups are dancing the dance. But don't take these communications as your cue to check out and start scrolling through messages on your phone. Whenever your pup is playing, it is your responsibility to monitor the games.

HEALTHY PLAY HAS A FEW TELL-TALE SIGNS. THIS IS WHAT YOU SHOULD LOOK FOR.[13]

SELF-HANDICAPPING:

This basically means that the pups are deliberately putting themselves at a disadvantage to indicate that play is welcome by doing things like rolling over to show the belly, lifting

---

13)   Skorobogatov, Maria. (March 8, 2014). The Differences Between Doggie Play and Aggression. NYC Doggies Urban Dog Wellness. https://nycdoggies.com/wellness/dogplay/.

their paws, and allowing their playmates to snatch the best toys. On the contrary, when dogs are feeling stressed or aggressive, their actions and body language will look tense and protective.

ROLE REVERSAL:

If Mikey is chasing Lola, and chasing Lola and chasing Lola, she is eventually going to feel cornered. In healthy play, Lola will chase Mikey, Mikey will chase Lola, Lola will take Mikey's ball then give it back, Mikey will chase Lola again, Lola will bark at Mikey then chase him, Mikey will mouth Lola's neck then give Lola the chance to chew his ears while he rolls on his back. The pups will literally reverse roles, frequently, and in many different forms of play as a way of communicating equal footing and good will.

ACTIVITY SHIFTS:

Healthy play will include all sorts of games and rests. The dogs will not only frequently reverse roles but will frequently mix up the activities from chase, to tug o' war, to wrestling and even mounting. They will be stopping to rest, to get a drink of water, or to check in with a parent.

Scuffles, barking, and even growling are all a part of healthy play, and things can get loud! If you are watching for and seeing communications of play, self-handicapping, role reversal, and activity shifts, even something that looks tough is probably just play. If, however, the games are dominated by one doggy, be on guard. Be watchful for signs of stress, like tail between the legs, yelps of pain, hair raised on the back, the tendency to cower, attempts to hide in tight corners, or attempts to get help from Mom by hiding between her legs. If the playful pup is not well socialized, she won't be able to read the cues being sent to her by the other dogs. That job will be yours. Finally, if you are just unsure, give it a test. Restrain the dominant dog if she is yours or ask her parent to do so if she is not, just for a moment. If the pup in question who was being chased comes running up for more, you know that the play is welcome. Let the games continue!

CHAPTER 15

HOW TO BREAK UP A DOG FIGHT

If you are vigilant when your pup is socializing, you should be able to read the signs of stress in most situations and nip any aggression in the bud before a fight breaks out. However, dog fights can happen anywhere, and the close quarters of an urban environment are particularly prone to creating the tense conditions that lead to aggression between dogs. Increased opportunities for socialization will naturally lead to increased opportunities for fights, but please don't let that deter you from taking your pup to the dog run. Instead, be prepared by learning how to decode play and by knowing how to break up a fight if and when it happens.

UNFORTUNATELY, MANY VISITORS to the dog park can neither prevent a fight by detecting the early signs of stress or stop a fight by safely intervening. In fact, it is often the parents themselves who elevate levels of stress at the park and make a bad situation worse. The recurring cast of characters should be familiar to seasoned dog run regulars. There's the high-strung parent with a sweet-faced, poorly trained, mid-sized pure-bred who believes his darling can do no wrong. At any sign of a scuffle, high-strung guy's nerves go into overdrive, and he instantly transforms the scene from dramedy to horror by making a lot of unhelpful noise from the sidelines.

There's the big dude with the really big unfixed dude-dog who tells everyone to chill out, perches himself in prime viewing position, and in his holier-than-though way announces that everything will work itself out, even when things turn bloody.

And then, of course, there's the angry one. This is the vigilante who, instead of helping to break up the fight, chases people around with a pitchfork blaming them for the aggression, the mess, and the bad weather.

The truth is, dog fights happen, they can be dangerous, and every dog parent should know how to properly handle the situation. If your dog is involved in a fight, whether or not she is the aggressor, it is never okay to aggravate the situation by panicking, to sit back and do nothing, or to incite hostility with the other parent by allocating blame instead of acting.

The best way to be prepared for safely handling a dog fight is to be familiar with

1) things you should never do,

2) the actions available to you for regaining control of the dogs, and

3) the situational variables that will determine what kind of action you need to take.

THE DON'TS OF BREAKING UP A DOG FIGHT:

Do not panic or scream.
Being agitated will only make the situation worse.

Do not try to separate fighting dogs by putting yourself or your hand between them, or by grabbing the collar.
Even if it is your dog who is acting aggressively and you think she would never dare to bite you, you are wrong! While engaged in a fight, dogs will bite whatever is within their reach, and placing your hand in the fight zone is extremely dangerous.

If only one dog is the aggressor, ***do not act on the dog being attacked.*** The aggressive dog will continue to attack, but you will have immobilized the other dog who can no longer defend herself. This is true especially with respect to picking up the dog in one's arms. Not only are you immobilizing her, but you are placing your body in the fight zone.

Do not run and hide.
If your dog is involved, you need to act.

Do not focus on the other parent.
Focus on safely resolving the fight between the dogs before picking a human fight.

If a dog is holding a bite on your dog, ***do not try to pull your dog from the other dog's mouth.*** You will cause an even greater injury to your dog by tearing her flesh. Act on the aggressor to make her release her bite.

THE DO'S OF BREAKING UP A DOG FIGHT:

The actions a person should take to safely prevent or separate a dog fight are described here in an order that is loosely applicable to ascending levels of aggression.

Use your voice and body language to regain control of your dog. This is usually appropriate before a fight actually starts, when the dogs are just posturing and displaying signs of aggression. Make a sudden noise like a very firm, loud "hey" or a strong clap of the hands to create a distraction; advance towards the dogs (but not in between them) and act tough in voice and posture; give your dog a warning nudge on her behind; if possible, do something unpleasant like spray water on the dogs.

If the dogs have begun fighting, grab the aggressor by her tail and pull up and backwards. When grabbed by their tail, most dogs will release a bite grip. Continue moving backwards, pulling the dog by her tail so that she cannot turn around and bite you. If you are not the parent of that dog, continue holding the dog by her tail until you can safely release the dog, grab the collar, or the parent arrives to take control of her.

If the aggressor dog does not release the bite grip when pulled by her tail, grab her back legs and flip her on her back.

Most dogs will release a bite grip when flipped on the back. It is very important that this is done correctly so that the action is safe and effective. Firmly grab one back leg with your opposite hand, while positioning the other hand on her croup. With an upwards sweeping motion, swiftly pull the dog's leg from under her, while pushing on her croup the other way. As soon as the dog is on her back, grab the other leg with your free hand so that you are firmly holding both of the dog's legs back legs. From this position you can control the dog so that she cannot bite you. Continue to hold and maneuver the dog until she stops putting up a fight, or the parent of the dog arrives to take control of her.

Under normal circumstances, the back-leg flip can be scary and unpleasant for a dog. However, when dogs are fighting, they are in a different psychological state, completely consumed by the adrenaline and aggression of the fight. In this situation, the flipping action is not traumatic for the dog; rather, it serves to remove her physically and mentally from the fight.

APPLYING THE CORRECT ACTION WHEN ONE PERSON IS BREAKING UP THE FIGHT:

In an "ideal" dog fight situation, both parents will act simultaneously and will know what to do. The parents will use the actions discussed above to gain control of their own dogs. Unfortunately, this is rarely the case. Usually, only one person takes action to separate the fight, and this person may or may not be the parent of one of the dogs involved.

If one dog is attacking and the other is defending and trying to get away, the person should act on the aggressor dog, using the actions described above.

If both dogs are attacking each other, it is best to try to separate them using non-physical methods. If you act alone and physically immobilize only one dog, the other dog will take advantage of the situation and could potentially hurt her. In most dog fights, after a few seconds, one dog will acknowledge he is weaker and try to get away. At this point one dog will become the aggressor and the other will become the victim. If the aggressor doesn't stop and goes in pursuit of the other dog, the person should take the appropriate actions (described above) to stop her.

In some cases, the victim dog may take advantage of the fact that the aggressor is immobilized and try to bite her. In this situation, if nobody is there to help, the dog being restrained should be released so that she can protect herself.

Dog fights can be very loud and very scary, and it is unfortunate that people often only make the situation worse. You can't stop Mr. Hysterical or Ms. Crusader but you can learn how to stop a dog fight. Familiarize yourself with these techniques, use a little common sense, and you will be able to keep yourself and your dog safe.

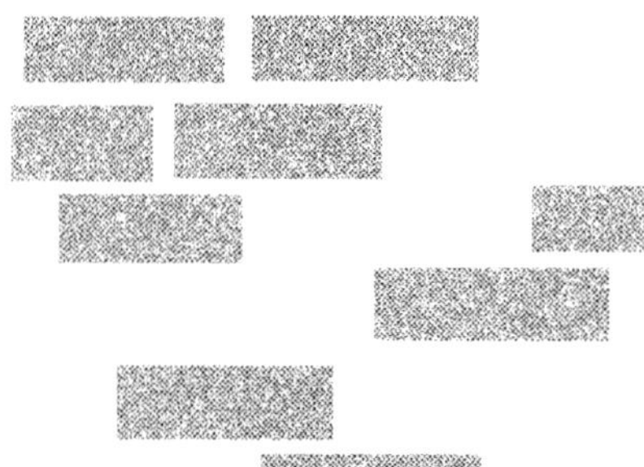

CHAPTER 16

HIRING HELP

Anybody moving to a place like New York will quickly learn that dog walkers and doggy care facilities are as integral to city life as taxis, food delivery, laundry services, and Bloomingdales. With subway commutes, long hours at the office, and a growing number of dual-income families, hiring help is a necessity for many urban residents.

LEARNING ABOUT THE SERVICES AVAILABLE can be an overwhelming undertaking because the safety, health, and happiness of your dog are at stake. The task is made more difficult by the presence of myriad dog services to choose from, all promising to be "the best" care for your pup. The information in this section is intended to ease that process by providing you with some basic answers to commonly asked questions about how the needs of your pup can be met by different services, i.e., how to hire a little help.

DO I NEED TO HIRE HELP?

Probably. For dog parents — city dwellers and suburban commuters especially — the minimum recommended amount of exercise for your dog of 3-4 hours is, in reality, aspirational. Most of us barely have enough time to go to the gym, and providing our pups with 4 hours of exercise every day can be unrealistic. Even taking them out in the middle of the day to poop and pee is impossible for most working people, and without some help your pup will probably be left alone in the apartment for long past the recommended limit of four hours at a time. Using a dependable and reputable dog service will provide your pup with exercise, mental stimulation, and fun, bringing you peace of mind and easing your busy schedule.

DOG WALKER VS. DOG DAYCARE

For most dogs, getting regular walks is a better option than daycare, with some exceptions. Dog walkers, if they are good at what they do, are better poised to facilitate an ideal activity schedule for your dog. Let us explain:

If a dog's environment is static, even if she is with other dogs she likes, she will get bored. While most pups have tons of fun playing at doggie daycare for about a week, this excitement quickly wanes and they become apathetic. Dogs need periods of rest, play, and stimulation with a change of environment at certain intervals. Scheduling walks when Mom or Dad isn't home will provide just this routine for your pup.

A topnotch doggie daycare facility would provide your pup with a cycle of rest and stimuli, would group compatible dogs together, would have outdoor space, and would be well-staffed. Almost none of them meet these requirements. That being said, for some people who work long hours, daycare is the more affordable option, and the social/interactive experience certainly beats being in an apartment alone all day. Some dogs who become anxious and aggressive on city walks do better in a daycare environment, as do some elderly dogs who need companionship but not much exercise.

CHOOSING A DOG WALKER

Choosing a dog walker or dog walking company is a tremendous decision for two reasons:

1) you are trusting someone you don't know very well with your beloved dog;

2) you are trusting that same person with keys and access to your home.

Reputation and *expertise* are of paramount importance in the search for a dog walker. It may seem like a job anyone can do, but to do it well and to do it safely, a dog walker needs training and experience. Talk to people in the neighborhood and don't be shy about asking for references. Local communities are a great resource.

Most dog walkers and dog walking companies offer different types of walks (see below), and you should choose one that best meets your dog's needs. Don't be afraid to meet with different dog walkers to see who you feel comfortable with — the best are in the business because they love dogs and are good at the job.

Using a dog walking service that carefully screens its dog walkers and that has been around long enough to build a positive reputation is usually a better choice.

WHAT DOES A DOG WALK ENTAIL?

TYPE OF WALK:

DOG PARK WALK: Many walkers take their doggies for a walk and then to a dog run or park in the neighborhood where the pups can play off leash. This provides the dogs with the chance to exercise, socialize with other dogs, and interact with people. As we have emphasized throughout this book, all of these things are extremely important in the life of a healthy and well-balanced dog. It is also a great way to become a part of the local dog community!

WALK ONLY: Some NYC dog walkers do not go to the dog runs, and instead take their dogs for neighborhood walks. This might be a good option for some dogs particularly if aggressive, but it is important to remember that a walk on the leash does not give your dog the opportunity to play and socialize.

The same can be said for another type of walk sometimes referred to as a ramble – dogs are taken on a long walk, in a circle around a particular neighborhood, dropping off and picking up other dogs along the way. This kind of walk is efficient for the dog walker, and does give your pup the chance to meet other doggies, but falls short of the kind of stimulation that a trip to the dog run or other off-leash play area provides.

OUT TO PEE ONLY: the most minimal kind of "walk" sometimes offered is for your dog to be taken out to poop and pee. Often, your dog will be picked up with several other dogs from the building, brought outside to go to the bathroom on the sidewalk, and then returned to the apartment. The disadvantages to this kind of outing are obvious.

PUPPY WALK: Individual walks specifically designed to meet the needs of young puppies (under 6 months old) are a wonderful option. A good walker will know how to provide appropriate care, exercise, and safe socialization during this vulnerable period before a puppy has all of her vaccinations.

GROUP SIZE:

An individual dog walk can be an appropriate option for aggressive, antisocial, or sick dogs. Some parents also just prefer that their dog be walked alone, whatever the reason. There are some very significant disadvantages to individual dog walks, however. Dogs are social animals, which means it is more fun and usually better for their wellbeing, to be walked with and to play with other dogs.

SMALL GROUP DOG WALKS, up to three at a time, are usually the best option. This allows the dogs to be social and get to know each other while ensuring that the dog walker can safely watch all dogs in the dog run. More than three dogs at one time is generally not a good idea and can be dangerous. Most dog runs set a limit of three dogs per person for this reason.

LARGE GROUP DOG WALKS are a sight to be seen. Veteran city dwellers may be able to impassively brush shoulders with crazies and celebrities, but the sight of a dog walker with fifteen dogs on a leash behind him will always turn heads. The scene is remarkable and iconic in New York and other cities, but large dog walks offer only one advantage: they are less expensive.

LENGTH OF WALK:

Many dog walkers in New York City take dogs for at least hour-long walks because it takes time to get the dog in and out of the apartment building and then to the dog run. An hour offers ample opportunity for the dogs to exercise, socialize, explore, and play (but most would stay all day if permitted!).

HALF-HOUR DOG WALKS are appropriate if your dog is elderly or less agile. That being said, we have seen plenty of barely mobile dogs happily relax and socialize in the dog run for hours on end.

For most dogs who are left home during the day, anything less than an hour is usually insufficient, and it is best if at least part of that time is spent off leash.

CHOOSING A DOGGY DAYCARE

If you decide that daycare is the best option for you and your pup, be aware that all daycares are not created equally because there is very little substance to the regulations. In NYC, dog daycare facilities are required to have a Small Animal Boarding Establishment permit and are regulated by the Department of Health and Mental Hygiene (DOH). In order to obtain a permit, the most substantive requirement is that a facility have one supervising manager who has passed an Animal Care and Handling course. Once opened, the facility has to inspect itself every two months for cleanliness, must obtain documentation of vaccinations for all of the dogs, and must provide an individual cage for each dog. While the DOH allows for common play areas, it does not regulate the number of dogs permitted in an area or the number of staff required for supervision.[14]

Most dog daycares found in big cities have a pretty straightforward structure and system. Dogs are grouped in rooms, often by size, and given cots, toys, water, and a supervising staff member. Most do not have outdoor space, but many do offer walks at an extra cost as part of the daily rou-

---

14) Article 161, NYC DOH Health Code.

tine. Typically, there is not a lot of social interaction between the dogs unless, as mentioned above, the environment and routine change throughout the day.

Choosing a daycare in close proximity to home or work is at the top of the list for most people, and we completely understand this need. However, we strongly recommend that you visit more than one option before settling on a place. To help in filtering your choices, we've included a list of things to look for and questions to ask when visiting.

OBSERVATIONS:

Are the dogs engaged in play?

Are the dogs in a relaxed state? Look for signs of anxiety like pacing and panting.

Is clean water visibly available?

Is the space ventilated (smelly)? Clean?

QUESTIONS:

What is the staff-to-dog ratio?

How are dogs grouped (size, energy levels)?

How many dogs per room?

Do the dogs always have access to a place to rest? To water?

Are there times when the dogs are closed in their crates? (This can be a good thing if part of a rest/exercise schedule, but not if used too much).

What kind of exercise and play are included?

Are staff trained in dog behavior (can they break up a dog fight)?

What is the protocol for emergency veterinary care?

HIKES

This is absolutely the best kind of exercise and fun a dog can get. In many suburbs and some cities like Los Angeles, natural environments, reservations, and hiking trails are easily accessible or even integrated into the urban landscape. A dog walk can actually mean a hike or an off-leash adventure because from pick up to trailhead is a matter of a few minutes' walk or drive. Lucky pups! For others, like NYC doggy denizens, getting into nature is not a simple proposition. Owning a car in the city is the first hurdle — most people don't because parking is difficult and traffic is a headache. Even if you do have a car, getting to a decent spot for a hike takes 60-90 minutes at a minimum.

Hikes are usually a day-long adventure that begins when pups are picked up in the morning, three or four in a group, then driven to a mountainous reservation outside of the city. The hike itself is a few hours of trails, grass, forest, and a lake or river for swimming. Regardless of size, age, or breed, pups are given an opportunity to do all the things they can't usually do in an urban environment like run off leash, swim, dig, track, and roll.

We highly recommend doing some local research to find out if there are any hiking services in your area, or if you live in an environment with easily accessible natural spaces, asking whether your dog walker ever uses them for regular walks. Of course, if you send your dog on an off-leash adventure, make sure she has a dependable response to "come," and check whether the company you are hiring uses any kind of tracking collars in case someone runs away.

WE ALSO SUGGEST ASKING THESE QUESTIONS:

How many dogs per hike? If it's more than four, it is not safe. When dogs are off leash, one person has to be able to quickly leash and gain control every dog in the event of an emergency. For example: unfriendly dogs belonging to someone else are encountered; someone catches a whiff of a squirrel and sprints; or, one dog trips and gets injured. The risks are there, and while we think the experience of being in nature absolutely outweighs the risks involved, safety is a huge concern. The best way for the dogs to stay safe is by keeping the group small.

How is the transport car set up? A group of dogs may

be the best of buddies on the trail, but when in the confined space of a car things are a bit different. A fight can occur if someone gets squashed or stepped on, even just scared or nervous. For this reason, dogs in the car should be separated by a barrier, with no more than two grouped together.

What are the emergency protocols? Hikers should have basic first aid equipment with them and should always have cellular phone service. In addition, it's important that the hikers are familiar with veterinary clinics local to the areas of the hikes. Finally, the company you hire will ideally have a back-up car and staff member to assist in case of a flat tire or other car troubles.

DO IT YOURSELF: GET OUT OF THE CITY

When possible, escape to the country! If you don't own a car, use a car share service (like Zipcar). If you can't drive, take the train! Every city has different rules, so do your research before showing up at the station with dog in tow, but there is usually a way. We've even seen hiking clubs for urban dog parents, and they help facilitate weekend, dog-friendly outings. If you live in the burbs, explore a little bit further afield on the weekend. Your pup will thank you.

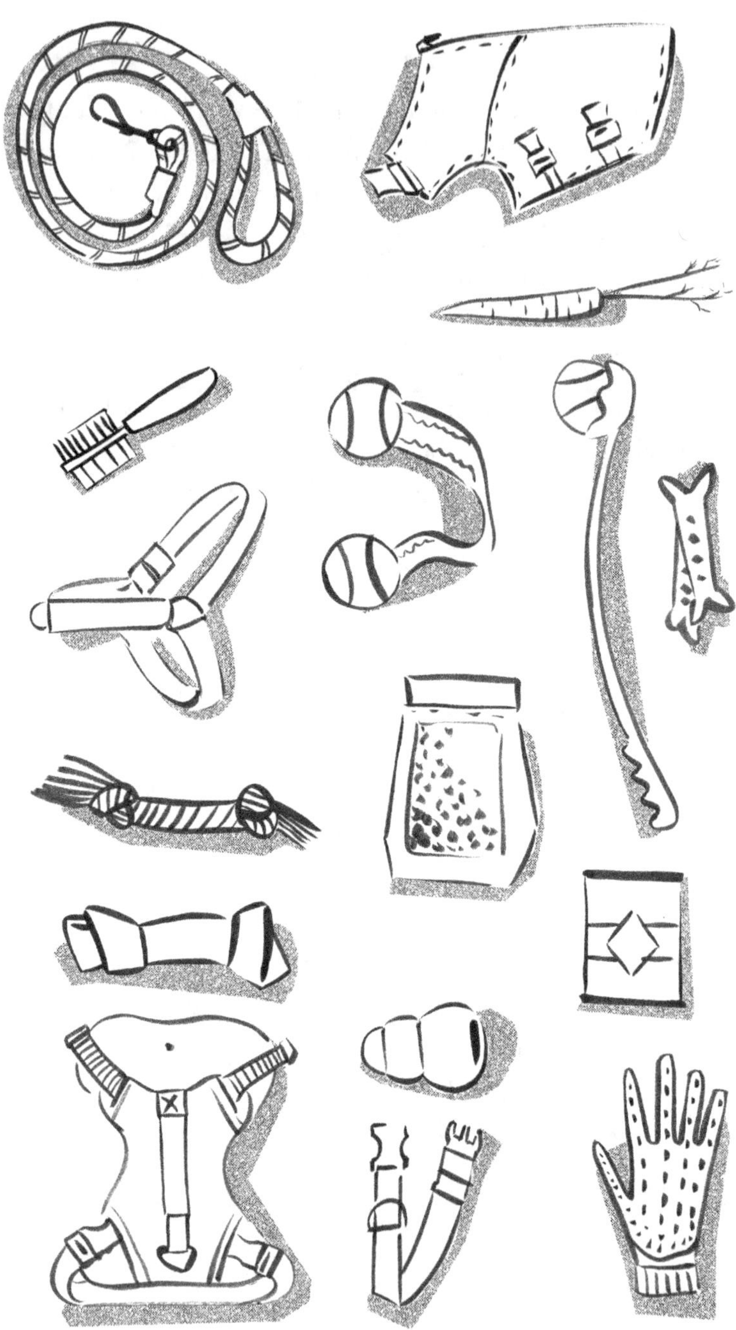

CHAPTER 17

GEAR

Many of our readers will be in the final stages of preparing to bring home a new puppy or adopted adult dog, and this preparation includes getting the gear you need. We suspect you may have already found yourself wandering the aisles of a pet supply store in overwhelmed confusion, parsing through rows and rows of collars, leashes, toys, treats, food, and everything is available in 3,000 colors, flavors, and materials. All of a sudden you are on your way home with a self-cooling dog bed, a coat for every season, and an empty bank account. Yikes!

WE ARE HERE TO HELP you navigate the world of dog gear. In this chapter we weed through the stuff that you really need, the stuff that you might need, and the stuff that you really *don't* need. We also address some very common misconceptions about gear, with a particular focus on different types of collars and harnesses.

The Barebones: when you bring your dog home, the absolute minimum that you need is a collar and a leash, toys, bowls for food and water, and basic grooming supplies. Ideally, you will have collars and leashes for different purposes, and you will probably want a bed for your pup. If you are bringing home a new puppy the essentials list will also include a pen, wee wee pads, and smell-eliminating cleaner for accidents.

COLLARS, LEASHES, AND HARNESSES

The rule of thumb to keep in mind when considering collars, leashes, and harnesses is that almost every design has a purpose for which it is well suited, but *problems arise when gear is used for the wrong purpose or used improperly for the right purpose.*

Your dog will wear a collar so that

1) she can be identified by the tags on it,

2) to keep her safe by having a place to attach a leash when you go for walks, and

3) to communicate a message to your dog through the collar by snapping the leash. Your dog will probably need more than one collar for different activities, and she may also need a harness.

Why You Don't Need a Harness for Everyday Leashed Walks:

Before we discuss specific types of collars, there is a dominating misconception about both collars and harnesses that needs to be put to rest. Many people believe that the gear will teach a dog not to pull on the leash. Wrong. *You* will teach your dog not to pull on the leash, and for guidance on how to do this please refer to the Obedience Training chapter. The reason we are taking the time to clear this up is because a lot of dog parents pick the wrong gear instead of picking the most comfortable solution (a collar) and properly training their dog not to pull. Some people opt for a harness because their pup pulls on the leash, and they feel that the harness is either more comfortable or more likely to change the dog's behavior. Neither of these things is true.

Right now, you might be thinking, "a collar pulling against her trachea is definitely more uncomfortable than a harness around her body." This may be right, but with a collar a dog can be taught to walk without pulling. Not so with a harness.

Why are we so sure your pup will pull in a harness? Because that is in fact what harnesses were created for. They were developed to encourage dogs to pull and lead and are appropriate for dogs who fulfill work that requires pulling like guide dogs for the blind, sled dogs, and tracking or police dogs. Harnesses specific to these jobs make it easier and more comfortable for the dog to pull.

Every year we see new and unimproved versions of harnesses being marketed to dog parents as the more humane choice for their pup. The result is a city full of dogs whose experience with a walk is, in fact, a battle with the harness. Instead of using the pulling instinct to complete a satisfying job, like sniffing out the drugs in a line of suitcases or leading Mom across the street because she can't see, the average dog in a harness is just struggling forward.

When said dog lunges at another pup passing by, Mom has no way of physically communicating her displeasure because any sort of snap of the leash will be barely felt and ineffectual. A collar will provide more control over your dog because a short snap of the leash can be used to clearly and quickly communicate to your pup.

We also see things like "gentle" leaders which attach to a dog's nose. To have something wrapped around your pup's muzzle is very effective: you can literally bend her neck anyway you choose, but this is incredibly uncomfortable for your dog. The same is true for harnesses that attach to the leash at a dog's chest instead of at the back — it is effective because if she pulls the harness her legs are virtually immobilized. She is not learning that she shouldn't pull on a walk, she just physically cannot.

This can be a good alternative to a collar for people who cannot teach their pup not to pull or need the extra help of gear to control a dog, for example, someone who is sick or frail.

All this being said, you may want to have a harness, even different types of harnesses, and your dog should be comfortable wearing them. While they are not the best choice for an everyday leashed walk for most dogs, they do have useful purposes.

First, if you want your dog to pull on the leash, for whatever reason, use a harness. Second, when your puppy is younger than five or six months old (before she is old enough to train), you will want to use a harness if she is a puller. You will use a collar sometimes so she gets used to the feel of it, but until she is old enough to learn how to properly walk on a leash, the harness will be more comfortable. Finally, if your pup is going to be running through the woods on a hike, you'll want to attach a tab leash to a harness (it's a leash that is only a couple of inches long), so that you can grab and hold her if you need to. In this context a harness with a tab or leash hanging from it will be more comfortable and effective than a collar. In addition, if your pup gets stuck on something in the woods, she won't hurt her neck when she pulls. Make sure that whatever harness you are using has an attachment for the leash at the back, not at the chest.

Hopefully we have convinced you to use a collar for normal, leashed walks, so let's get to it!

TYPES OF COLLARS:

Collars are usually made with either leather, metal chain, nylon, polymer nylon, or a combination of those materials, and they come in four designs: basic, martingale, prong, and slip. All collars should fit snugly, but not tightly, around the dog's neck when placed under the chin at the bottom and behind the ears at the top. The collar should just make contact with the skin all the way around without drooping or hanging, but it should not be pinching your dog's skin.

The BASIC COLLAR is just a circle that fits around your dog's neck. It shouldn't dangle or squeeze. It is the appropriate choice for most dogs who are well behaved, who walk without pulling on the leash, and who don't need a strong correction. It is also appropriate for a dog who is often free to roam outside off leash. It won't dangle and get caught on anything but will be in place for identification purposes.

The MARTINGALE COLLAR has a large loop which goes over the dog's head and a smaller loop that the lead is attached to. When the leash is slack, the collar fits comfortably around the dog's neck, but when the leash is pulled the collar tightens. When fitted properly, it is impossible to choke or strangle your dog with a martingale collar. For off-leash roaming, martingale collars can be problematic if the second loop (usually attached to the leash), hangs. Particularly for smaller dogs, the martingale is prone to getting stuck on things like tree limbs when off leash.

The SLIP COLLAR is also known as a choke collar. The loop tightens when the leash is pulled, but unlike the martingale collar there is no limit to how tight it can go. The slip collar is our least recommended design because of the obvious dangers of strangling, but like most gear it does have an appropriate use. For a well-trained dog who doesn't pull on the leash, the slip collar is the most un-intrusive for everyday use. Like a martingale, the fit of a slip collar is really comfortable for your pup when she is just hanging out at home, but the materials for a slip collar can be make it lighter and more minimal than a martingale. This is the absolute put-on-and-forget-about-it collar, particularly if made with long, fur-saving chain links.

The PRONG COLLAR has a set of evenly distributed prongs or studs that lie on the inside of the collar around a dog's neck. While it is not the best everyday collar for most dogs, it is a tool that can be used appropriately. We'll take a minute here to briefly address fears about prong collars because there is a lot of readily available misinformation.

A prong collar, if used properly, will not be putting a constant pressure against a dog's neck. It will be attached to a leash that is slack, only tightened for a quick, momentary correction. The quick pinch paired with voice will grab a dog's attention when needed, but the leash is immediately slackened again. Naysayers claim that the prong collar is cruel and painful, and they demonstrate this by putting the prong collar around a person's neck and asking how it feels. Does it feel great? Absolutely not, but let's dig a little deeper. What the naysayers never do is put a basic collar around a person's neck, pull with a constant pressure against the trachea, and then ask how that feels. Take our word for it, the basic collar feels terrible too. But remember, your dog will be taught to walk without pulling while wearing a collar.

If she is wearing a prong collar and does start to pull, the pressure is actually more evenly distributed around her neck because of the prongs, and therefore less likely to damage the neck or trachea. However, the only time we really recommend using a prong collar (because of the risk of improper use), is during the proofing phase of training with a dog who is not very sensitive. This provides a quick, clear, and efficient way of communicating to a dog with a larger or stronger neck during training.

Prong collars should really not be used as an everyday collar, and if you do use one, make sure it is fitted properly and check regularly for loose links. We often see dogs wearing prong collars inside out for everyday use, and we advise against this. When the prongs face outward, they can injure other dogs during play.

TYPES OF LEASHES:

You will need three different sized leashes for your dog.

The first is your everyday walking leash, ***standard length is 6 feet.***

The second is a ***15- to 30-foot-long training leash.*** This should be relatively lightweight because it is going to be hanging from your dog's neck. The training leash is long because it provides a tool for control at a distance with a dog who is not fully trained.

The third leash you will have is just a ***few inches long and is called a tab.*** The tab will attach and hang from your dog's harness. This is used during the later stages of training and for a trained dog when you are on off-leash walks. It gives you a way to grab and hold her if needed.

RETRACTABLE/EXTENDABLE LEASHES:

We said that most gear has an appropriate use, but the scope of use for an extendable leash is extremely limited. In general, we do not like them, and we do not recommend them. These leashes are prone to accidents, give you very little control over your dog, and are dangerous to other dogs and people.

The effect of a retractable leash is to be constantly taught. With a continuous pressure on your dog's collar, you have very little control because you cannot communicate to your dog by snapping the leash. In addition, your ability to bring your dog closer to you depends on a very undependable plastic button and some odd maneuvering.

Extendable leashes are made from a thin, almost wire-like rope because it has to be small enough to retract into the handheld container. There are two problems with this material. The first is that if you ever need to grab the rope to gain control over your dog, you will cut your hand. Likewise, if your dog becomes entangled (and she will, because extendable leashes provide so little control), the rope can cut or strangle the other dog or person.

The only time we think it is okay to use an extendable leash is if you have a small dog that needs to be leashed because she does not have good recall and you are walking in the countryside or a secluded environment with no other dogs present.

COLLAR AND LEASH MATERIALS:

LEATHER is great for both leashes and collars because of its versatility and flexibility. Leather leashes provide the best "snap" when you need to communicate with your pup, and they are comfortable to hold.

We love rolled leather for collars; the round profile is not only comfortable but is less damaging to fur than flat collars. The downside of leather is that it does degrade with heavy use, particularly if your dog swims a lot.

NYLON leashes and collars are most commonly flat in profile (this is called nylon webbing) but can also be found in a round profile (nylon rope). Nylon is both strong and inexpensive, so it is by far the most common material found in leashes and collars. As with rolled leather, we like nylon rope for collars because it is better for the fur around the neck. Nylon leashes do not snap as effectively as leather, and the material does get dirty quickly. If your dog is an avid swimmer and hiker, be prepared for a smelly collar.

POLYMER COATED NYLON is basically nylon webbing or rope coated in plastic. This is a great material for dogs who like to get wet and dirty. They wipe clean, hold up well to wear and tear, and don't get stinky.

METAL is heavy, and we do not recommend it for a leash, but metal does have a place in some collars. Prong collars are usually made from it because of their specific shape, and some slip collars are made with long, fur-saving links. In addition, metal chain is very effective as the second loop on a martingale collar because of its ability to slide easily against whatever material is used for the primary loop around the dog's neck.

Be thoughtful when choosing the material for your leash and collar. Don't get heavy braided leather for a Pomeranian because it will weigh her down. Likewise, a thin nylon leash probably isn't the best choice for a bull mastiff! In fact, when shopping for leashes and collars, we recommend going to a physical store with your pup so that you can actually see, feel, and try out different options. You can keep it local in New

York and other cities where independent shops have even created their own brands and gear specifically designed for urban pups.

PUPPY SUPPLIES

In addition to a leash and collar, you'll need a few important basics when you bring home a new puppy:

A Pen. This can really be anything used to create a space for your puppy to stay when she is unsupervised. We like metal, foldable puppy pens.

Wee wee pads. You'll need a lot!

Toys. Unless you want your dog to be a lifelong shredder, get toys that are difficult to destroy.

A Bed. It's important that your puppy has a space in the pen for sleeping that is distinct from her place to pee and poop.

Cleaning supplies. When you are housetraining your puppy, it is important to clean up accidents with something that kills the odor.

Bowls for Food and Water.

CRATE:

Like all dog gear, crates have appropriate uses, and many

urban residents will want to have them. However, we do not recommend them as a housetraining aid. Crates are the ultimate inhibitor when it comes to pooping and peeing because puppies will do their best not to go where they sleep. We advise against this approach to housetraining because you will not be setting your puppy up for success. You can read more about why in our Puppy Training chapter.

Your dog should be familiar with and unafraid of the crate because you may need to use one for travel, and because at some point in her life she may have to stay overnight at a veterinary clinic where she will be crated. You may also want to crate your dog if she is destructive and cannot otherwise be contained when unsupervised. A large-breed puppy who regularly jumps out of the pen to chew furniture and empty the garbage, for example, would ideally have a safe room to stay in, but we recognize this is not always possible. The crate is another alternative for keeping her safe.

In the case of travel, crates are often necessary, especially if you are going to be traveling by airplane. For travel by subway, bus, taxi, and even boat, you'll be able to bring along a small breed dog in a crate or other carrier. Being mobile with your pup is a wonderful thing, and cities offer so many modes of transportation.

You won't need to crate your puppy every day, but you will need to introduce the crate or carrier occasionally and at a young age so that she gets used to and comfortable in it. Another solution is to leave the crate open in the pen with your puppy so she has regular access to it. When the actual day of travel arrives, the last thing that you want is to introduce your dog to the additional stress of being in the crate for the first time.

Be sure your crate is the proper size for your dog. She should be able to stand up, turn around, and lie down, but you don't want extra space because she will be more likely to soil the crate. Never crate two dogs together.

A NOTE ON POOP DISPOSAL

On this front, suburban and city pooches are certainly united and likely envious of their rural comrades who get to poop freely in the woods without being tugged, watched, and cleaned up after. The very natural act of defecating becomes oh-so-unnatural in the urban environment, and parents must be prepared with a system of poop disposal. Most people walk their dogs with a little pouch that contains a roll of bags specifically designed for picking up poop and putting it in the garbage.

While this is a great system for keeping our sidewalks clean, we would not be upholding the spirit of this book if we simply left it at that. Plastic bags are an environmental menace; please consider using alternatives when possible:

BIODEGRADABLE BAGS: These are better than regular plastic bags, but please read the fine print. Most require special composting conditions.

POOP SCOOPER: Many dog runs have scoopers or shovels for collecting poop and putting it in the garbage can. Please use these instead of a bag when possible.

TRASH: Whatever it is that you are already throwing away, could it be used to pick up poop? Yes, this is a question we regularly ask ourselves. Whether it is a plastic bag from produce at the grocery store, an empty potato chip bag, or the wrap from a sandwich, that's one less bag for the landfill, and one less thing to buy.

FLUSH IT: when your puppy is still pooping on wee wee pads in the house, why use a bag at all? Pick it up with toilet paper and flush it.

HEALTH AND GROOMING

MILD SHAMPOO. Unless you are treating a specific skin condition, most dogs do best with a very mild shampoo. What you don't want to do is strip your dog's coat of all its natural oils. Her skin will become dry and irritated.

NAIL CLIPPERS. Not all dogs will need to have their nails trimmed; often very active large breeds' nails wear down on their own. For others, there are a million and one choices. We suggest sticking with something simple. More important than having fancy clippers is getting your puppy used to the process when she is young.

BRUSH. Again, this is breed dependent. For those that shed

a lot we love brushes that tackle the undercoat. For hair that clumps up, a de-matting comb will be useful. And for dogs with short hair, a soft-bristled brush is enough to get rid of debris.

EAR CLEANER. Not all dogs will need this, but many will. Choose a mild formula and consult with your veterinarian if you notice that your pup has itchy or sore ears.

FLEA AND TICK PREVENTION. You can discuss a monthly application of a formula that is applied to the skin or, now, taken as a pill. Other options are special collars and sprays for the fur.

HYDROGEN PEROXIDE. If your dog eats something potentially toxic, you will always first call the ASPCA poison hotline. They will likely recommend giving your dog a dose of hydrogen peroxide to make her vomit, so always have some on hand.

SOFT CONE OR INFLATABLE TUBE. Whether it is a simple hot spot or scrape or she is recovering from surgery, at some point your dog will likely need a cone. Have a soft cone and an inflatable tube (it goes around the neck) at home.

BOWS, BOOTIES, AND OTHER ACCOUTREMENTS

If, after reading this book, you still think All That Glitters is going to contribute to the health, happiness, and good behavior of your dog, we have not done our job.

We think this is a good place to come full circle and reflect on perhaps the most important principles that buttress our approach to parenting an urban dog: celebrate and understand the dog, in all her dogginess, while tuning out the noise, the gimmicks, the quick-fixes, and the accoutrements; don't anthropomorphize her behaviors because doing so will diminish your ability to meet her actual needs; ditch the raincoat (dogs have their own) and the embellished water dish, because what your pup needs from you is lifelong practice and understanding.

Remember, whole dog parenting is not about molding canine behavior to the demands of the urban environment. It is about adapting urban life to meet the natural needs of our dogs. In doing so, we set the foundations for successful training by ensuring that our pups are happy, healthy, and balanced.

ON ILLNESS, DEATH, AND LIFE

Two months after Emma died, I took the rough draft of this book to meet with my friend Julie, an author and fellow dog-lover. The previous summer, Julie had said goodbye to her dear Maggie, a beloved pup who battled chronic intestinal illness for three tough years. Maggie was a dog who nuzzled her way into everyone's heart. Ovidiu had cared for her since she was a puppy, and she was the first dog (other than my own) who I took hiking nearly ten years ago.

MAGGIE WAS AN INTELLIGENT, energetic, affectionate, troublemaking, shepherd mix, and we loved her. Over the course of our dogs' lives, Julie and I regularly got together to chat about the latest writing projects we were each working on and inevitably ended up sharing stories about our naughty, food-driven pups: the devilishly cute ways that Emma and Maggie accessed anything edible from opening cabinets to chewing through dashboards.

On the day I brought the book to Julie, however, we couldn't help talking about having watched our sweet girls die. We were both still reflecting on and recovering from the experience of caring for an infirm dog, of trusting a veterinarian to properly guide us, and then ultimately having to decide the moment when our dogs would take their last breath.

With Emma, our veterinarian had come to our home, and Ovidiu and I were able to say goodbye with our girl in my arms. Emma's decline had been rapid — her body was riddled with tumors, she was in pain, and it was clear when it was time to let her go. For Julie, watching Maggie fight for life and then finally die was a much longer journey, three years of ups and downs and hope and pain. Maggie was young when she first became ill, just seven years old. She suffered from an intestinal disease that causes protein loss, and it slowly took her life.

Alongside the bounty of joyful memories, illness and death have been ever present in recent conversations with Julie about our pups. So, when reviewing my manuscript, we were both surprised by its absence. How had I completely bypassed this important component of dog parenthood? How had I failed to write about what it really means to adopt, as a wonderful part of one's family, a being whose natural lifespan is shorter than our own? It turns out that I, like most parents, experts, advice-givers, and veterinarians, am practiced at avoiding the most inevitable truth of dog parenthood: mortality.

I have certainly experienced it — not only in death, but in the everyday ups and downs of life. Emma was a regular at the emergency vet clinic in Brooklyn. She had a hernia, a slipped disc, pancreatitis, various growths and tumors, and once got her paws on a box of raisins. Her lifetime medical bills totaled roughly $15,000. Ollie and Azzy have been luckier in comparison, though not without sick visits.

Through it all I learned that deciding the right course of treatment for one's dog involves weighing a number of factors: a dog's age and overall health, the probability of success, potential side effects and risks, and of course, silently hovering at the forefront of Mom or Dad's mind, the expense. A vet once said to me, "I know you would sell your house for your dog, but this expensive treatment might not be the right course of action." At the time I didn't own a house, but I thought, "Oh yeah, I would definitely sell it if I had one." Looking back, that would have been a crazy thing to do. The vet probably didn't actually expect me to sell my house, but time and time again I've been faced with expensive treatments for my dogs, and often the veterinarian asserts that the right choice is to proceed with treatment, regardless of financial, physical, and emotional cost.

One of the most difficult aspects of dealing with illness in dogs is that the best course of action is rarely clear. When Emma was 12 years old, she woke up one morning unable to walk. Our regular veterinarian had recently moved, and the emergency clinic staff did not understand that the difficult decisions we would make regarding Emma's treatment were based on a complicated history. A few years before, in fact, the day I went into labor with our first child, Emma had undergone an extensive surgery to remove a tumor from her chest. So much tissue was removed that it was more than a year before Emma physically recovered. I decided that at her age, she should not undergo another such intensive procedure if more tumors appeared (and they did).

The emergency veterinarian suspected that Emma's sudden paralysis was caused by intervertebral disc disease, a ruptured disc that was putting pressure on her spinal cord. They would keep Emma overnight and perform surgery in the morning. The assumption was clear: I had to opt out of the procedure, not in. When I pushed for information about alternative treatments, Emma was sent home with a course of steroids, and I was instructed to return in a couple of days if they didn't help.

Three days later, with Emma still unable to walk, we returned to the hospital because if the steroids were going to work, we would have seen results. I gasped when the veterinarian handed me a $7,000 surgery estimate. Like most dog parents, I want to do whatever it takes for my pups, but resources are finite. The question of just how much money one should spend on medical — particularly end-of-life — care for dogs is so personal, so complicated, and so often avoided. I was lucky to have some clarity in making the decision for Emma; her body could not handle another surgery. However, when the vet suggested that instead, they could humanely euthanize her that very day, I left with Emma in a fog of tears, self-doubt, and anger.

The next evening, Emma regained mobility in her back legs, and she was able to walk and run, with the occasional wobble, until her death one and a half years later.

Things may or may not have been easier with a veterinarian who knew Emma's history, but having an established relationship is an important way to prepare for facing illness and making difficult decisions about treatment. And all dog parents face difficult decisions, struggling with hard questions of medical treatments under the real or imagined judgment of their canine community. Medicine is often a complicated inquiry, and when Mom or Dad and the doctor are in the process together, when there is trust between them, and when questions are encouraged, outcomes are better. That is the kind of relationship Julie has with her veterinarian, and it was the basis for attuned medical care that extended the length and quality of Maggie's life. When Maggie first became ill at seven years old, everyone was stumped by the symptoms. Eventually, she was diagnosed with Intestinal Lymphangiectasia, a disease that causes protein loss through the intestinal tract. In true partnership, Maggie's veterinarian, specialists, and Julie's family monitored Maggie's symptoms, adjusted her medications, and adapted her treatment to provide Maggie with the fullest life possible for three more years.

Julie has an adorable new pup named Frankie, and in a beautiful way, Frankie's sweet and silly temperament honors the memory of her predecessor. She is similar physically, a medium-sized shepherd mix, and she shares Maggie's affectionate personality and intelligence. But in other ways she is so very different, and the differences cannot help but conjure up memories of the one who came before her. It somehow feels like Frankie has been adopted into a home that was shaped in a most loving way for her, by Maggie.

In our last meeting, Julie and I agreed that the death of

our dogs remained near. I still see phantom images of Emma, a movement of white in my peripheral vision that stops my heart because I think for a moment that it is her chubby, wagging tail. Emma's absence is palpable. For my daughter, at almost four, losing Emma was her first experience of death. Bea is particularly saddened by the fact that Ollie needs to be closer to us now, at all times, because his sister died. She understands his loss because she has a little sister; they sleep in the same bed together just like Ollie and Emma did.

When it was time for me to go home, Julie reiterated that this conversation about mortality and illness and money and old age and medical care — all the things nobody wants to think about or talk about — needed to be shared. Of course, she was right. Perhaps because we expect our children to outlive us, most of us are wholly unprepared for the fact that we will outlive our dogs. We will raise them with love, we will share in joyful moments, we will nurse them when they get sick, and we will hold them when they die.

Before leaving Julie's house, I looked down at sweet Frankie, curled on the floor, and reached over to give her head a scratch. She opened one curious eye and gave a satisfied wag of her tail before drifting off to sleep again. "How do we bear it?" I asked Julie.

"Because they teach us so much about how to live," she replied.

And so they do.

DOG BREEDS

If your energetic pup is nipping at the heels of children in the park (likely a shepherd), digging holes in your furniture (a terrier perhaps), or barking incessantly at the dog run (scent hound!?), there is probably a very good explanation for her behavior.

IT'S ALWAYS A GOOD IDEA TO RESEARCH the dog breed that you own or the breed you are thinking of getting, and there are plenty of good resources on offer. Dog encyclopedias are a great first stop for basic information about traits, purpose, and history of specific breeds. But what we have found to be missing is a guide that helps parents navigate breed traits within the reality of the environment in which we live (*hint — it's not the environment most dogs were bred for). We also want to encourage readers to be thoughtful and realistic about their own limitations and expectations for a four-legged companion. Your dog should be compatible with you and your lifestyle, not just cute.

Most people in the United States who own a dog live in a city or suburb, and even those who live in rural areas primarily own dogs as companions, not as working dogs. Pair this with the fact — with very few exceptions — that dogs were bred for a working or sporting purpose, and the conditions are ripe for unexpected or unwanted behaviors. What we aim to do in this appendix is provide a little context and guidance on what to expect and how to best manage the behaviors that often pop up as a result of this misalignment: dogs bred for a specific purpose living in a permanent state of urban retirement. In addition, we'll cover some breed traits that are surprisingly adaptable to city and family life.

If you are the proud parent of a mutt or designer mixed-breed pup, this section is absolutely still for you; it may be even more important! Every mixed-breed dog is the result of a love affair between dogs bred for a specific purpose even if the pure-breed rendezvous happened a few generations ago. Gaining some insight on the different pieces that contribute to the whole puzzle of a personality can be helpful in navigating the behavior of any dog.

We aren't going to address every breed here, just those groups most commonly owned, and our aim is to be broad enough to cover the most prevalent breed-specific issues. Our hope is that no matter what breed or mix you own, we will give you enough tools to be able to think about behaviors from a different perspective — as something that may be deeply rooted in your pup's DNA. That being said, it is also important to keep in mind that absolutely every single dog is different, personalities not only differ at birth but are heavily shaped by the environment in which a dog is raised. Breed traits are not absolute, they are just one useful piece of the puzzle.

RETRIEVERS

(Most popular: Labrador and Golden)

Retrievers, by far the most common being Labrador and golden retrievers, are sporting or 'gun' dogs, which means they were bred to be used in hunting. Historically, hunters have used dogs for a diverse range of purposes: spaniels for flushing game out, setters and pointers for locating game, hounds for tracking, and retrievers for, you guessed it, retrieving game!

This means that despite their reputation for being sweet family dogs, retrievers were bred to be working dogs, and they will only thrive if given the opportunity for a lot of outdoor exercise. Ever seen a goofy-looking lab jumping into a pond over and over again to fetch a ball or a stick or a rock or a leaf or whatever happens to be available? That's because it's in their DNA. Retrievers usually love water because they were expected to retrieve game, like ducks, from the water once it was killed or wounded. They also tend to have gentle mouths which are a necessary trait for bringing birds or game undamaged by teeth back to their parent.

Retrievers are keen swimmers, and their coats are designed to keep them warm in the water. This means that they have a lot of hair, usually an undercoat for warmth and a top coat for keeping water off of the undercoat and skin. This hair sheds a lot, particularly when the seasons are changing — maybe not a plus for apartment living.

On the other hand, Golden and Labrador retrievers have a reputation for being great at obedience training and very willing to please. Of course, dogs are all different, but given proper social conditions and early training, the foundations for a well-behaved and sociable dog are there. Retrievers tend to get along well with kids, but they also tend to get along well with strangers, so don't expect a guard dog!

TIPS FOR CITY LIVING: These are dogs that will tirelessly fetch at the park or dog run, so take advantage! Not all breeds can be exercised so efficiently in virtually any environment. Remember to give your retriever a chance to swim whenever possible.

POODLES

Do not be fooled by the pretentious-looking hairdos donned by show poodles; these dogs have grit and are anything but ornamental. They come in three sizes: standard, miniature, and toy. Poodles are highly intelligent, easily trained, and very athletic, traits that have made them an extremely versatile breed used for hunting, guarding, and companionship. Their incredible agility and trainability historically made them great circus dogs, but this was not their original function. From the German *Pudelhund,* or water dog, poodles were bred as sporting 'gun' dogs with much in common with retrievers. They worked closely with parent to retrieve fallen game during a hunt, often from the water.

One defining difference between poodle and retriever is

the coat. Instead of a double layer of underfur and top coat, poodles have curled wooly hair that repels water. Poodle hair produces less dander than most dogs and sheds slowly, which is one of the reasons for its popularity.

But poodles aren't just popular as poodles. This Adonis of canines, with amazing hypoallergenic coat and incredible intellect, has been used exponentially more than any other breed to create new "designer" hybrid breeds. Cockapoo, labradoodle, goldendoodle, schnoodle, maltipoo, peekapoo, and shipoo are just a few poodle mixed breeds. The fact that specific traits of the poodle (like hypoallergenic coat) cannot be guaranteed in the mixed offspring has not deterred these designer breeds from taking off in popularity. And why not? Oodles of poodles are wonderful, so long as parents are prepared to care for an athletic and energetic companion, not an ornamental lap dog.

TIPS FOR CITY LIVING: Poodles and poodle mixes adapt well to city life, though they need rigorous exercise.

SHEPHERDS

(Most popular: German Shepherd Dog)

The most popular shepherd in the United States is the German shepherd dog (GSD), but some other common shepherd breeds are the border collie, Australian shepherd, and old English sheepdog. All shepherds were initially bred for gathering, protecting, and herding livestock. It is not an easy undertaking. Just imagine the complex balance of abilities needed to successfully herd a group of animals such as sheep! It is a task that requires acuity, intelligence, trainability, and athleticism, and all shepherd breeds at their origin were very carefully selected for these traits. No other group of dogs is more naturally attuned to their parents which makes sense, given the nature of herding work. A working shepherd dog is outside with shepherd parent, engaged in an incredible dance-like duet, constantly moving, watching, taking subtle cues, and reacting in step to keep the herd safe.

It is this intelligence and ability to take specific guidance from a trainer or parent that has made shepherds, in particular the German shepherd, extremely adaptable to other kinds of work. The GSD is used as guide dog for the blind, guard dog, and performs a variety of jobs for policework such as protection and explosive or contraband detection.

Shepherds need an enormous amount of exercise and mental stimulation to maintain their health and happiness. In an urban environment, the results of not providing the proper activity level to a shepherd can be disastrous and heartbreaking. Imagine a dog whose genes are telling her to be outside running, to be keenly aware of her surroundings, and to learn new things from her parent, being kept most of the day in a city apartment. Pent-up energy, as in all breeds, can lead to destructive behaviors, but the psychological effects can be far worse, particularly for a breed that is thirsty for stimulation. Boredom might start out as pacing and eventually lead to intense anxiety. Shepherds are dogs who want — and need — to perform active, interesting tasks. If you are looking for a simple companion dog to take for a leashed walk a couple of times per day, a shepherd is not for you.

Shepherds tend to enjoy learning new things (training), games, and athletic challenges. They are great with activities like agility courses because being constantly engaged with their parent comes naturally. This attunement — the trait that was selected for over centuries for herding livestock — is a big responsibility. In addition, shepherds require a lot of time outside. They were made for it (literally)! They usually have a lot of hair with an undercoat to protect them from the outside elements, and this also means they shed a lot and require regular brushing. A shepherd is not for the inactive or aloof parent, nor is a shepherd the right dog for someone who has allergies or can't stand pet hair.

TIPS FOR CITY LIVING: However you exercise your shepherd (and she will need A LOT of exercise) make it mentally stimulating for her as well. She needs you to be engaged and will thrive with proper training. Think about specialized training to meet her intellectual needs!

TERRIERS

(Most popular: Yorkshire Terrier)

Terriers are tough, energetic, independent, brave dogs originally bred to hunt and eradicate vermin and guard the home. These dogs are great at digging and following prey into burrows (terrier is the modern French word for burrow, and terra is Latin for earth). They are also highly reactive to movement or anything out of the ordinary in their environment — think about a working terrier sitting on her stoop, waiting for the slightest movement to indicate a creature that needs killing.

Yorkshire terriers (Yorkies) are by far the most common breed in this group, and while they may look like the perfect teeny tiny urban apartment dog, they are in fact 7 pounds of extremely tough terrier tenacity, originally bred to kill rats in English clothing mills. This is not a submissive lap dog, but a very protective and highly reactive terrier. Yorkies were expected to be attuned to their environment for the most subtle warnings of unwanted pests.

While their size and perky demeanor are often alluring for city dwellers, do not be fooled by the cute factor of a Yorkie if you are looking for a quiet family pet. They are smart and quick to learn, but all terriers need a lot of mental stimulation and physical activity. The high level of reactivity is not always great when children are involved, and biting is a problem we see quite a lot of. If dealt with properly and immediately, Yorkies respond very well to training, but parents tend to ignore or overlook bad behaviors because of their small size.

TIPS FOR CITY LIVING: Our best piece of advice for people who own a Yorkie or any other terrier is not to treat this dog as a lap dog. Behavioral problems in this group often stem from parent expectations of a small dog being mismatched with breed traits. Give your Yorkie lots of activity, mental stimulation, and outdoor off-leash exercise. Let her dig, run, bark, chase, and roll in the park so that she doesn't dig, chase, and snap in your home.

HOUNDS (MOST POPULAR, BEAGLE)

For hounds it is all about the hunt! With some overlap, hounds can be broadly grouped into scent hounds and sighthounds. Scent hounds have powerful noses and were bred for tracking game at a slow and steady pace with parent following. Sighthounds are fast and follow prey by keeping it in sight. We are going to focus on scent hounds because they are much more common in the United States than sighthounds, the beagle being far and away the most popular.

We adore hounds (after all, we have two of our own — a basset hound and a dachshund), so we can fairly say with love in our hearts that these guys are not the most obedient and not very easy to care for in an urban environment.

Scent hounds have an independent quality to them because they need independence to do the job they were bred for. Unlike shepherds and retrievers who are constantly in communication with their parents on the job, scent hounds are expected to follow prey for long periods of time, on their own, with stamina and endurance but without checking in with Mom or Dad until prey is quarried. How does a parent know where to find said hound? By following that unmistakable hound bark, of course.

The loose lips and floppy ears that many scent hounds come equipped with are designed to help catch scents, but to many parents they complete the squishy and oh-so-adorable package. Beagles, bloodhounds, and basset hounds, to name a few, can be pretty darn cute and gentle, but parents or prospective buyers should be realistic about how scent hound traits will or will not jive with life as an urban companion dog.

Scent hounds bark. It's in their DNA, and it is fun. Our Basset hound Emma earned the moniker of dog run "sheriff" based on her reputation for barking at and chasing, at a leisurely pace, any and all dogs running in the dog park. And barking. And barking. Unfortunately, the instinct does not turn off once inside an apartment. If you need a quiet dog, a scent hound is not for you.

Scent hounds are not always easy to train. That independence necessary for the hunt makes them seem . . . stubborn, but do not let that fool you into thinking they aren't smart. Blind obedience is merely one type of intelligence. A scent hound will always win in a contest of how-do-I-get-the-box-of-cookies-off-the-shelf.

TIPS FOR CITY LIVING: Do not let perceived lethargy fool you! Scent hounds are slow, and often pretty squishy, but they are dogs bred for a job of endurance, and they need a lot of exercise. Outdoor exercise and activity will also help temper the barking indoors. Off-leash exercise can be tricky with hounds because they are made to follow their noses without looking back, so always be cautious. Tracking activities are a favorite with hounds, and on rainy days these dogs can be easily entertained in the house with a game of hide-the-treat.

DACHSHUND

According to the American Kennel Club, dachshunds are scent hounds, but we've placed them in their own category because behaviorally (and genetically) they are really a combination of scent hound and terrier. Dachshunds track prey by scent but also chase by sight and are excellent at digging and tunneling as they were originally bred to catch badgers. That long and short wiener shape actually has a purpose! Imagine these tough little sausage dogs digging their way through tunnels and ferreting out quarry. In addition to athleticism and instincts to track and dig, dachshunds have a stubborn streak, or as some like to say, they are independent thinkers. This, in fact, would have been a necessary trait for a dachshund on the job, making decisions in an underground tunnel without the benefit of receiving communications from parent.

TIPS FOR CITY LIVING: This popular breed is adored by New Yorkers and residents of other cities, but we see a lot of behavioral problems that likely stem from incongruity between parent expectations of a lap dog and the reality that dachshunds are tough, athletic hunters. Dachshunds require physical activity, mental stimulation, and firm boundary setting. Without this, they are very susceptible to being antisocial with other dogs, stubborn, nippy, and overweight.

BULLDOGS, FRENCH BULLDOGS, PIT BULLS

All dogs that were bred to bait bulls, including bulldogs and pit bulls, have a dense, muscular build, wide stance, and wide mouth. Why? Because they would have been expected to actually fight a bull. With a strong, stable body, the dog was able to lunge at the bull's head then grab onto the bull's nose with her mouth and remain attached while the bull flung its head from side to side. Despite this rather grim and cruel history, bulldogs' loving personalities have allowed them to become one of the most popular companion dogs in the country. The squat, squishy English bulldog is the most popular nationally, while the French bulldog takes the lead in cities like New York. Pit bulls don't make the list statistically, but we think there are many more pit bull parents in reality that report the breed as something else because of the aggressive stigma. We'll talk a bit about these three breeds, though there are many more in the bull-baiting category.

BULLDOG

Since bullbaiting was outlawed almost 200 years ago, bulldogs have been selected for gentle, family-friendly temperaments. They are generally mild mannered but not known to be easy to train. One of the most important things to think about when considering getting a bulldog is their health and lifespan. They are prone to many diseases and have a short lifespan. If you aren't prepared to deal with serious skin, eye, spinal, and other health issues, this is not the dog for you.

FRENCH BULLDOG

French bulldogs were bred by mixing bulldog with terrier. These little pups are sweet and very cute. French bulldogs have a good average lifespan, but like standard bulldogs, they are prone to a host of genetic health problems. In general, they make good apartment dogs because of moderate exercise needs, limited barking, and love of human companionship.

PIT BULLS

Though pit bulls were originally bred by combining bulldog with terrier, that is about where the similarities with French bulldogs end. Despite the stigma, pit bulls are not inherently more aggressive than terriers or other breeds. Like any big, strong breed they are not for everyone and require proper training, exercise, and socialization.

From droopy-jowled hounds to tenacious terriers, this list of popular urban dog breeds covers the full range of canine personality quirks. By looking past the fluff, we hope we've provided you with some insight as to which breed traits are compatible with your lifestyle and home environment. Just remember that nature plays a part, but no matter what kind of dog you decide to bring home, nurture is more important. With proper socialization, care, training, and lifestyle choices, any pup can be a happy, healthy, well-behaved urban dog!

MOST POPULAR BREEDS LIST
BY AMERICAN KENNEL CLUB

Nationwide Ranking[15]

1. Labrador Retriever
2. French Bulldog
3. German Shepherd Dog
4. Golden Retriever
5. Bulldog
6. Poodle
7. Beagle
8. Rottweiler
9. Pointer (German Shorthair)
10. Dachshund

NYC[16]

1. French Bulldog
2. Golden Retriever
3. Labrador Retriever
4. German Shepherd Dog
5. Bulldog

---

15)   Reisen, Jan. Most popular dog breeds of 2021. American Kennel Club, 2021, https://www.akc.org/expert-advice/dog-breeds/most-popular-dog-breeds-of-2021/.

16)   AKC staff. Most popular dog breeds by city 2021. American Kennel Club, 2021, https://www.akc.org/expert-advice/news/most-popular-dog-breeds-by-city/.

CHEAT SHEETS

LIFESTYLE GUIDELINES CHEAT SHEET

A well-behaved dog must be happy, healthy, and balanced. The only way to achieve this is by taking a holistic approach to raising your pup, which means you are providing socialization, exercise, activity, nutrition, and proper health care.

Without these components of a healthy lifestyle, training is moot.

SOCIALIZATION:

> Socializing your pup means showing her that she will always be safe in your care when experiencing the vast and diverse world that you live in. Dogs must be socialized with other dogs, people, environments, and sensory experiences.
>
> Socializing with other dogs is critical even for pups who appear to prefer the company of humans. Walks, visits to the dog run or park, and play dates at home are all good ways to give your dog opportunities to interact with her species.
>
> Dogs can react with fear or anxiety to those that don't look or smell or move like Mom or Dad if they haven't been properly socialized with different types of people. Invite people to your home, visit other homes, go out into the city and the parks talking to and interacting with people of all shapes, sizes, ages, and colors; uniformed and glasses-wearing; hatted and helmeted; bikers and skateboarders; and importantly, children.
>
> Socializing to different environments means that your pup will learn to love both nature and the excitement of urban life; she will be happy in the quiet environment of home or on the noisy train; and when faced with unfamiliar sights, sounds, or smells she will respond with curiosity rather than fear. Take her everywhere, let her smell everything, and show her how to safely experience new places with you by her side.

EXERCISE AND ACTIVITY:

Mind and body need to be fit. Dogs who don't get enough physical and mental activity are more prone to behavioral problems and cannot be easily trained.

> Natural behaviors like rolling, sniffing, chewing, digging, and barking can be destructive or "icky" in a domestic, urban setting, so give your pup appropriate opportunities to express these behaviors.
>
> Get out of the city and let your dog explore clean, natural spaces off leash. Let her run, dig, swim, track, roll, and bark.
>
> When in the city, make sure she gets to the dog run or off-leash

hours in the public parks.

In the home, stimulate your pup with activities like hide-and-seek, an obstacle course, obedience training, or just a big bone!

NUTRITION:

All commercial kibble and canned foods are more or less nutritionally equal, even the expensive, organic ones. They all have to meet the same AAFCO (Association of American Feed Control Officials) guidelines, and the processes of canning and kibbling are great levelers when it comes to the "fresh" ingredients listed on the packaging.

Beware of marketing gimmicks and use a critical mind when choosing what to feed your pet.

A fresh and varied diet can be the most nutritious and enjoyable food experience for your pup. Consult the AAFCO and NRC (National Research Council) Nutrient Requirements for Cats and Dogs publications to make sure your dog is getting what she needs.

Fresh meat, bones, vegetables, fruits, and grains can make a delicious and balanced home-prepared meal for your pup. An animal-protein focused diet is usually the best way to meet nutrient requirements.

Keep your dog lean. A heathy weight is the real nutritional magic bullet!

HEALTHCARE:

Pick an experienced veterinarian to be the primary caregiver for your dog. Your vet will keep your pup up to date on vaccinations, flea, tick, and heartworm prevention.

Know where you can take your dog in case of a medical emergency.

Keep some basic supplies at home like hydrogen peroxide, sterile bandages, and a cone.

Keep your dog well groomed — teeth, nails, ears, skin, and coat.

Consider pet health insurance and microchipping.

HOME-PREPARED MEAL IDEAS

If you have decided that home-prepared meals will constitute some or all of your pup's diet, we've compiled a list of a few of our favorite recipes to get you started! We cook for a big family, and by using whole meat sources and vegetables, we keep it economical and nutritious.

CHICKEN, BROWN RICE, AND BROCCOLI: Instead of buying just the chicken breasts or legs, pick up a whole chicken, gizzards and all. We cut off the parts we like to cook for ourselves and the kids, then chop the rest of the bits up for the dogs. We serve it with cooked brown rice, and broccoli. The florets go to the humans and the dogs get the stalks, cooked or raw! The meat and organs constitute the main part of this meal, with a smaller serving of rice and veg.

SALMON AND SWEET POTATOES: It doesn't have to be expensive! None of our two-legged family members eat the nutrient-rich skin, so after we have grilled the salmon, we peel off the skin and give it to the dogs with cooked sweet potatoes.

BEEF AND CARROTS: We often pair these ingredients together, whether it's in a stew or a roast. For this type of cooking, inexpensive cuts are delicious. We buy large cuts and trim them ourselves. The pups get the raw trimmings, any leftover stewed meat, and of course the delicious carrots, raw and cooked.

** Some Foods to Avoid **: chocolate, grapes/raisins, onions, garlic, macadamia nuts, foods high in fat, alcohol, cooked bones, foods with tough rinds or pits, xylitol (often found in gum). This is a nonexclusive list. When preparing a homemade meal for your dog, always check that the ingredients are safe for canine consumption first.

FOUNDATIONS OF TRAINING CHEAT SHEET

TAKE A HOLISTIC APPROACH: Set your pup up for success. You cannot expect her to be balanced and well behaved, let alone learn to obey commands, without first meeting her needs for overall wellbeing. Exercise her body and mind, teach her how to enjoy interacting with the world in a social way, keep her fit and healthy.

PRACTICE: Training is a lifelong commitment for both you and your pup. You will need to practice so that you can effectively communicate with your dog, and your dog will need regular practice to maintain the good habits and commands that you teach her.

MATCH VERBAL LANGUAGE AND TONE WITH BODY LANGUAGE AND ACTION: Clear communication is essential. If you want your pup to understand that "no" means "no," you must tell her with a firm voice and matching posture, even a snap of the leash. Likewise, if she has done something great don't just tell her; show her that you are pleased by giving her affection. Please do not use affection to calm or soothe your pet when she is displaying signs of anxiety or aggression. The message being received is that the behavior is wanted.

BE CONSISTENT: This is another type of clear communication. Unwanted behaviors or the failure to follow a command must elicit an appropriate, consistent response from you every single time.

ACT IMMEDIATELY — TIMING IS EVERYTHING: Rewards and correction must be offered immediately because dogs live in the Now. A few seconds can be the difference between a "good girl" that your dog links to peeing on the wee wee pad and a "good girl" that she links to chewing on your shoe, which is what she started to do after she peed.

KNOW MOTIVATION, INCENTIVES, AND CONSEQUENCES: Every dog is different, and it is your job to figure out what drives her to act and what consequences are meaningful. She will be motivated by food, toys and play, affection, or all three. She might be sensitive to just your voice when she misbehaves, or she may require something more like a tap on the nose. Training will be most effective once you understand your pup's individual personality and preferences.

DO NOT HUMANIZE YOUR DOG'S EXPRESSIONS AND BEHAVIORS: Anthropomorphizing your pup is doing her a disservice. Dogs are amazing creatures in their own right, and by approaching situations from a dog's perspective, you will be better able to understand what is going on and to communicate clearly.

BE THE BOSS: Don't let your dog rule the roost. If you want her to get off the sofa, she must get off the sofa, and if you sometimes want her to be next to you it's fine to invite her up. House rules should never be dictated by your pup, especially if she tries to get her way with expressions of aggression like growls and snaps.

BE AWARE THAT CUTE PUPPY BEHAVIORS ARE OFTEN NOT CUTE ADULT BEHAVIORS: Everything is sweet when your puppy is small — chewing, jumping, barking — but not so sweet, sometimes even dangerous, when she grows up. Remember that habits formed as a puppy will persist into adulthood.

PUPPY TRAINING CHEAT SHEET
THE ROAD MAP:

NO OBEDIENCE TRAINING: From when you bring your puppy home, to around 4 to 6 months of age, you and your puppy will be getting to know each other, socializing, and learning the house rules. Obedience training can wait.

SOCIALIZATION: Between 8-16 weeks, nothing is more important than socializing your puppy. This is it! If you socialize your pup properly in this window, you are setting the foundations for a well-behaved adult dog.

> Socialize her with other dogs. Before she is fully vaccinated only socialize in safe, clean environments with dogs you know and trust to be healthy and friendly. This will lay the foundations for a balanced, happy pup who can interact with friends.

> Socialize to different environments and people.

> Socialize to handling and gear. Get your puppy used to your touch, the collar and leash, being walked, held, poked, and prodded. All of these physical interactions will prepare her for necessary health and grooming like ear cleaning, tick checks, and visits to the vet.

LANGUAGE: You will learn your puppy's language, and she will learn yours.

> First, get to know your puppy, particularly through play. Play also sets the foundations for training.

> Second, introduce your puppy to three clear messages:

> *Praise* — express to your puppy that you are happy with what she has done without being over excited. Pair a warm message like "good girl" with toys, affection, or treats.

> *Displeasure* — use a firm voice, dominant posture, and short word like "hey" to express that she is not supposed to do something. Use the minimum firmness needed to convey your message while still being effective. You don't want to scare your puppy.

> *Neutral commands* — you will be asking things of your dog in a casual way by using phrases like, "let's go." Your voice will be calm, casual, clear, and neutral.

> Keep your vocabulary minimal, repetitive, and consistent.

> Don't rely solely on your voice.

HOUSE RULES AND GOOD HABITS:

SAFETY: You will be supervising your puppy when she is not in her pen, but please make sure that your home is nonetheless safe — we are all human and there will be times when you aren't paying attention. Put cables, cleaning supplies, chocolates, anything toxic, and anything life-threatening out of reach.

WHAT TO CHEW: Chewing is normal. Your job is to teach her what she can and cannot chew.

Step 1: Purely positive training. Both in the pen unsupervised and out of the pen supervised, your puppy will only have access to things she is allowed to chew. Use play to encourage her to chew appropriate toys. If she finds something inappropriate like the corner of the rug, redirect her with a toy. Toys should not be destructible.

Step 2: When she is familiar with toys and play, after a few weeks you can introduce the gentlest possible correction for chewing something she isn't supposed to. A short "hey" sound of displeasure should be enough, but if it isn't, you can pair it with something slightly uncomfortable like pressing your finger on her tongue or picking her up by the scruff of her neck. Immediately redirect with positive play. During this stage, she is still supervised at all times when not in her pen.

Step 3: Your puppy gets more and more freedom in your home as she becomes better acquainted with the rules. By the time she is a few months old you will remove the pen altogether but be smart and keep dangerous items tucked away.

HOW TO PLAY: Yes, this is an important skill and good habit! It helps set the foundations for a positive relationship, clear communications, developing skills, and lifelong learning. You will use play to introduce motivating factors and the concept of obedience training.

You must work to engage your puppy and keep her attention by showing excitement and rewarding good play. Treats, affection, praise, and play itself are all good rewards.

Practice games like chase-and-retrieve, tug o' war, and running.

JUMPING, EXCITEMENT AND WHINING: Discourage these behaviors because your pup will not always be so small! Do so by modeling calm and quiet behavior when you get home. If she jumps on your leg, push your knee or foot outward and she will stop. Give your puppy a few minutes to relax before you show her affection. Whining for attention should be ignored and not rewarded. Attention is given when your puppy is in a relaxed state.

SEPARATION: Separation takes practice and you will start as soon as you bring your puppy home. You will teach her that being alone is not scary but comfortable, and the best way to do this is to exercise her before leaving. Feed her, take her for a walk, play and engage with her, then leave her to curl up and sleep. When she wakes up you will be home and associations with separation are positive.

WALKING ON A LEASH: During these early weeks you will be getting your puppy used to the concept of walking on a leash. You will use collars and harnesses to take her for daily walks, being sure to keep her engaged. Do not use corrections for pulling at this stage.

HOUSETRAINING:

You will teach your puppy to use wee wee pads and to go outside, gradually reducing the pads until she is always peeing outside.

GEAR AND SPACE:

> When you bring your puppy home you should have a pen prepared. This is an enclosed space big enough to hold a wee wee pad, a bed, toys, food, and water, at least 5 feet by 5 feet. This is where your puppy will be when she is not supervised.
>
> You will have wee wee pads strategically placed around the house where your puppy can easily access them at all times.
>
> You will have cleaning supplies for accidents.

You will get your puppy on an eating schedule as soon as possible, and she will eat at least 3 times per day until she is older. Water should always be available. She will need to pee frequently, and she will start pooping on a schedule, usually after eating.

Throughout this process, you will be vigilantly supervising your puppy when she is not in her pen.

> ***Stage 1: Introduce the concept of a proper place to pee and poop.***
>
> Your puppy knows nothing and will have accidents. Introduce the concept of where to pee and poop: 1) place her on the wee wee pad as soon as you see her start to go, and 2) reward her when she goes on her own in the proper place.
>
> You are not communicating displeasure at this stage.
>
> Do not startle her when you pick her up to move her to the wee wee pad, and do not offer praise if she finishes peeing or pooping on the wee wee pad after you move her.
>
> Do offer praise when she goes to the wee wee pad on her own or outside on her own, but wait until she is finished so that she is not startled or interrupted.
>
> ***Stage 2: Begin eliminating wee wee pads.***
>
> From within a few days to a few weeks your puppy will begin using wee wee pads most of the time. Remove them one at a time, beginning with those least used.
>
> If she starts having accidents, replace the most recently removed wee wee pad.
>
> Throughout this time get your pup on a walking schedule. Her in-

stinct to go outside will kick in and patterns will form. When she understands the concept of where to poop and pee (she gets it right 85% of the time), you may begin making her slightly uncomfortable when she has accidents by picking her up with a light pressure under the armpits and tilting her body while moving her to the wee wee pad. This is not painful. Do not use a tough voice, she will startle.

Praise is still used consistently when she goes outside or on the pad.

Stage 3: Your puppy is anywhere from 3 to 5 months old, and she is housetrained.

At this point you have one wee wee pad left in your house, probably by the front door, and your pup is almost always peeing and pooping outside.

You may now use a gentle vocal expression of displeasure like "hey" when you pick her up if you catch her in the middle of having an accident.

Your feeding and walking schedules are aligned with her need for peeing and pooping.

When your puppy stops using the last wee wee pad, get rid of it!

SETBACKS AND PROBLEMS:

If your puppy seems to be learning the rules but starts having accidents, you may be moving too fast. Take a step back — usually this means reintroducing a wee wee pad and making sure you are supervising her with vigilance.

Regressions and accidents are more likely if your pup is not getting enough outdoor exercise.

A fully trained puppy who then starts having accidents could be sick or reacting to something in her diet. Check with your vet.

If your puppy is chewing wee wee pads when unsupervised in her pen (this should never be happening under your supervision), first make sure she has something better to chew, and if this doesn't work, fix the pad to the floor.

GETTING RID OF THE PEN:

When your puppy knows where to poop and pee and knows the house rules, she will be ready to have free reign in the house when you are not there to supervise.

OBEDIENCE TRAINING CHEAT SHEET

PREPARATIONS: You will begin obedience training when your puppy is about 6 months old, and dogs at any age over 6 months can also learn obedience. In order to prepare for training your puppy you will

> Have a relationship with the dog you are training.
>
> Understand what motivates your dog.
>
> Practice and effectively communicate with words, tone, and body language three things to your dog: praise, neutral commands, and displeasure.
>
> Revisit the Foundations of Training chapter.

POSITIVE TRAINING AND ENFORCEMENT:

> New concepts are always introduced and taught in a positive manner.
>
> Once a new concept is understood, enforcement is used to demand obedience when your pup disobeys (during the proofing phase, see below).
>
> ***Enforcement has 3 steps:***
>
> 1) When your pup disobeys, you will get her full attention by communicating displeasure with your voice and tone, and, if necessary, with a snap of the leash.
>
> 2) You will enforce the command through physical manipulation. If she didn't come when you called, for example, you will take the leash and immediately walk her to the spot at which you were standing when you first gave the "come" command.
>
> 3) You will immediately practice the command again.

THE PROCESS: The three stages of obedience training are ***Teaching***, ***Proofing***, and ***Maintenance***. We use "come" and "sit-stay" as examples.

> Start by establishing a relationship with your puppy through play. Play is also how you will get your puppy's attention and practice effective communication.
>
> Prepare to spend *one hour training every morning*, followed by multiple 5-10-minute training sessions throughout the day.
>
> Begin training in a quiet place, outside, with few distractions.
>
> Begin with a long 15-30-foot leash on your dog, then gradually work your way to a 6-foot leash and then a tab (just a few inches) as she gets more reliable in her response to your commands.

Teaching: New commands are introduced using positive reinforcement. Your dog learns to associate a word and a gesture with a specific desired action, and she begins to respond reliably when the command is given in a quiet, controlled environment.

1) Introduce the action and associate the action with a verbal command, gesture, and reward.

In a simple and comfortable environment, use play to get your dog to move towards you and to sit. For example, run backwards and encourage her to follow; lift a treat above her head to encourage her to take a sitting position.

Begin using a word and a gesture for each command when your dog is performing these actions. Reward and praise her each time she comes towards you and sits.

2) Begin using the command.

As your dog makes the connections between the commands and the actions, you will begin using the command before she performs. If she is ready, she will follow your commands, and you will provide lots of praise and amped-up rewards when she does.

Play, practice, and repeat.

Always watch for signs of stress and fatigue.

Proofing: The command is tested in different environments, with more distractions being introduced, one at a time, until your dog has mastered the command and reliably responds.

Baby Steps: incrementally make the environment more distracting. The first step is a little bit of distance between you and your pup. Introduce either a new setting or new distractions in one training session, not both at the same time.

One Distraction at a Time: Never introduce more than one new distraction or level of difficulty at a time. Once a distraction is mastered it can be paired with another distraction that has also already been mastered independently.

Enforcement: In the proofing phase, you will enforce obedience when your pup doesn't respond to the command.

Intermittent Rewards: Once your dog has mastered the concept and is responsive in different environments, alternate when you give your puppy a reward.

Maintenance: Daily, lifelong practice. Integrate ways to practice all obedience commands in everyday life and play.

CITY LIVING CHEAT SHEET

DOG PARK ETIQUETTE:

The dog run is a hive of social activity that requires rules and etiquette to avoid combustion! Be considerate, attentive, and thoughtful of other patrons. This is a communal space, where toys are shared, poop is picked up, messes are made, and civility is key. Don't bring kids or food, do open and close the gates one at a time.

LEARN TO RECOGNIZE HEALTHY PLAY:

>A well-socialized dog will learn how to play, but not all dogs know the rules! Some dogs cannot read the signs, so it's your job to be attentive and knowledgeable.

>Healthy play will include: body language like the "play bow," ears back, licking, paw-raising, whining, and grinning; puppy-like movements; self-handicapping; role reversal; and, activity shifts.

>Healthy play is often loud and rough. Don't interfere but do pay attention.

>Redirect at the first signs of stress.

KNOW HOW TO BREAK UP A FIGHT:

Do not panic or yell. Do not try to separate dogs by putting your hand between them. Do not focus on the other parent. Do not focus on the dog being attacked.

Do

>1. Use your voice and body language to regain control of your dog before the fight has broken out.

>2. If dogs have begun fighting, pull aggressor by her tail, up and backwards. Pull her away from the fight and continue holding until she has calmed or until parent takes control of her.

>3. If aggressor does not release bite, grab back legs and flip her on her back.

GEAR:

>Must haves: collar and leash, toys, bowls for food and water, basic grooming supplies.

>When bringing home a new puppy, you will also need: a pen, wee wee pads, and odor-eliminating cleaner.

>Health and grooming supplies should include mild shampoo, nail clippers, brush, ear cleaner, flea and tick prevention, hydrogen peroxide, and a soft cone or inflatable tube.

>Crate: it's a good idea if you plan on travelling with your pup.

INDEX

FURTHER RESOURCES:

Visit our website for more information, videos, and articles about the topics covered in this book. All of our work is the product of original, in-depth research. We remain unbiased, and we do not offer advertisements or sponsor any outside products or services on our blog.
www.wholedogparenting.com

ABOUT THE AUTHORS:

Jennifer Wheeler, J.D., is a graduate of New York University School of Law, writer, and co-owner of NYC Doggies. She has lived and worked all over the world, including in Thailand, Nepal, Ecuador, Switzerland, and The Hague. Her previously published work focuses on politics and democracy, and she is also the creator of the NYC Doggies Urban Dog Wellness blog. jenniferwheelerauthor.com

Ovidiu Stoica, M. Eng., earned his Master of Engineering degree from the Mircea cel Batran Naval Academy in Constanta, Romania before moving to New York in 2002 where he founded NYC Doggies (nycdoggies.com). Ovidiu has been a dog trainer for over twenty-five years, applying his background in the sciences to developing an effective, results-based methodology for training urban dogs. Ovidiu and Jennifer have been married since 2015, and they have two daughters together.

Oana Stoica is a visual artist and art director based in Romania. She created the illustrations and cover for *Whole Dog Parenting*. Her portfolio can be viewed at teacept.com.

9 798218 086107